LIVING
AGAINST THE
GRAIN

Other Books by Tim Muldoon

A Saint for All Reasons

Come to the Banquet

Longing to Love

Love One Another

Seeds of Hope

Six Sacred Rules for Families (with Sue Muldoon)

The Ignatian Workout

The Ignatian Workout for Lent

LIVING
AGAINST THE
GRAIN

HOW TO MAKE DECISIONS
THAT LEAD TO
AN AUTHENTIC LIFE

TIM MULDOON

LOYOLA PRESS.
A JESUIT MINISTRY
Chicago

LOYOLA PRESS.
A JESUIT MINISTRY

3441 N. Ashland Avenue
Chicago, Illinois 60657
(800) 621-1008
www.loyolapress.com

Cover art credit: © Catherine MacBride/Stocksy United

ISBN-13: 978-0-8294-4503-9
ISBN-10: 0-8294-4503-X
Library of Congress Control Number: 2017930453

Printed in the United States of America.
17 18 19 20 21 22 23 Bang 10 9 8 7 6 5 4 3 2 1

AS KINGFISHERS CATCH FIRE

As kingfishers catch fire, dragonflies draw flame;
As tumbled over rim in roundy wells
Stones ring; like each tucked string tells, each hung bell's
Bow swung finds tongue to fling out broad its name;
Each mortal thing does one thing and the same:
Deals out that being indoors each one dwells;
Selves—goes itself; myself it speaks and spells,
Crying Whát I dó is me: for that I came.

I say móre: the just man justices;
Keeps grace: thát keeps all his goings graces;
Acts in God's eye what in God's eye he is—
Christ—for Christ plays in ten thousand places,
Lovely in limbs, and lovely in eyes not his
To the Father through the features of men's faces.

—Gerard Manley Hopkins, SJ (1844–1889)

CONTENTS

PROLOGUE

This is a book about passion—about living a life with roots sunk deep into soil teeming with life, so that all we do bursts forth beauty. The secret—hardly a secret—is that beauty is really never about something out there but rather is a quality of seeing, a quality of living in the everyday that enables you to see something that can break your heart.

I think you know what I mean: perhaps you too have had glimpses of that kind of beauty when you've been moved to wonder, tears, or surprise. It has nothing to do with magazine definitions of beauty, or even travel guides to beautiful places. It has to do with an appreciation of the reality of the world, an insight that may be hidden from others but whose meaning captures you and reminds you that the world is a far greater and more wondrous place than we allow our time-crunched selves to recall.

I watched a video recently made by a college student who had returned from a months-long immersion in El Salvador. Like many of my students who have served abroad, he was searching for the right superlatives to explain his time there: it was "amazing," "heartbreaking," "unbelievable." His video, meant to capture some of what he had experienced in working with residents of a small village, focused on the faces of the men, women, and children: they were playing games, cooking, working in the field. There was laughter;

there was running into the waves of the ocean; there was shared food, conversation, and even photobombing. In a word, there was nothing extraordinary—just ordinary life. And for the young man, there was God.

What did this young man learn to see there? What was happening beyond the events of an average day? What enabled him to see life differently?

For many years I've taught a senior capstone course at Boston College called Desire and Discernment, which is rooted in St. Ignatius of Loyola's *Spiritual Exercises*, a powerful compilation of meditations, prayers, and practices. That course, from which this book takes its inspiration, is an invitation to students to learn how to see: to take "a long, loving look at the real," to quote the words of the late theologian Walter Burghardt, SJ. Over the years, students have shared stories with me of how they've come to see the world differently. Sometimes it's because of a significant relationship, one that stretches them to see through the eyes of their beloved instead of their habitual way of seeing. Sometimes, like the young man in the video, it's the result of experiencing a new culture, where they encounter real poverty for the first time and start to think critically about their habits of consumption. Other times it's the result of a trauma, like the death of a loved one or the divorce of parents—events that upset their everything-happens-for-a-reason optimism.

Invariably—even among those students who joke that they are "ruined for life" (a common plaint among former members of the Jesuit Volunteer Corps)—the response to this "learning to see" is gratitude. For at the heart of their experience is a new sense of self: a new sense that—to quote the words of the poet Gerard Manley Hopkins—"what I do is me," not some plastic shell of a self that imitates others in a race to nowhere. These students begin to experience themselves as gifts and their lives as paths of discovery that open up new relationships, new hopes, new desires.

Perhaps you too have a lingering sense that your life is destined for more. Perhaps you, like so many of my students, feel the desire to live your life in a way that is more than going to work, making money, having fun, then rinsing and repeating. If that is the case, then I invite you to practice discernment, that capacity by which we come to discover our truest selves and how to make a difference in the world. And in so doing, we'll discover a God who is very much alive in our service to others.

A POETIC IMAGE

Gerard Manley Hopkins, a Jesuit priest whose name is included in the "Poets' Corner" of Westminster Abbey, along with other great English poets, gave profound language to this new form of seeing. His poem "As Kingfishers Catch Fire," which appears in the front of this book, beautifully captures the promise at the heart of this seeing. He meditates on five things that catch his senses: a bird flying low over a lake, a dragonfly reflecting the sun, a stone being thrown down an old well, a string plucked on a musical instrument, and a bell tolling in a distant church tower. All these things, he says, do one thing: they are themselves.

> Each mortal thing does one thing and the same:
> Deals out that being indoors each one dwells;
> Selves—goes itself; *myself* it speaks and spells,
> Crying *Whát I dó is me: for that I came.*

What does he mean? Consider Hopkins's use of the word *selves*. It's a verb form of the word *self.* Each thing selves when it does what it is created to do. And for Hopkins, human beings too have the capacity—like the bird, the dragonfly, the stone, the musical instrument, and the tolling bell—to selve by most truly being ourselves. That is our natural state—a state I see children practicing without thinking when they are at play. Selving is what happens when we allow ourselves the freedom of children at play, letting what's inside of us to shine forth. Too often, our fears and anxieties hold that beauty within, denying the world the opportunity to behold something good that God has made. Hopkins nudges us to be aware of this tendency, to recover the natural beauty of selving, and to live unafraid.

> *When do you selve?*
> *When are you most yourself?*
> *Are you aware of it when it happens, or do you become*
> *   aware of it later?*
> *Are there things in your life that get in the way of selving?*
> *Do you find it easy to discern a sense of your deepest self, or*
> *   does that feel like something distant from you?*

However, we are often mysteries to ourselves, and so selving becomes complex. St. Augustine's autobiography *Confessions* is a reflection on the difficulty of coming to understand himself. He narrates the movements in his life that led him to freedom in the Christian life, detailing along the way how hard it was to know what he should want. After the death of a friend, for example, Augustine was overcome by emotions that he could not understand: "I had become to myself a vast problem." Life throws many things at us. We experience emotions and passions that make us question where we are going. Life is risky. And at any time in our lives, we are presented with options that were unthinkable a generation or two ago, let alone in the premodern world, when most human beings lived and died within miles of their birthplace. There is something almost frightening about stopping to take a long look at the real: it might become overwhelming. Can we look honestly at the state of our relationships with those we love? To see all the ways we have failed to love or failed to let others love us? Can we take the time to assess how well we live justly and the extent to which we instead focus on our immediate needs? Can we train our eyes to see those whom Jesus pointed out in his ministry—lepers, prostitutes, tax collectors, and other sinners? Too often we are content to keep our head down and go along with the flow of getting and spending, entertaining, working, living, dying.

Yet if we are honest with ourselves, even in the midst of the getting and spending, we mysteries unto ourselves are cauldrons brimming over with competing desires.

> *How are we to selve?*
> *What will enable us to preserve our name in the pages of the*
>   *world's history book?*
> *What work shall we do?*
> *What hobbies or activities will refresh us?*
> *Which people shall we keep in our hearts?*
> *Which relationships will bring us joy?*
> *Which causes will we give our time and money and*
>   *sweat to?*
> *Whom will we go out of our way for?*
> *How should we leave the world a little bit better for our*
>   *having been in it?*

These are towering questions, and like the author of the book of Psalms, we may feel that "such knowledge is too wonderful for me, far too lofty for me to reach." (Psalm 139:6)

The insight that is at the heart of this book is one for which I claim no originality, for it is as old as the psalms and the gospels. For the psalmist, God was nearer than the next breath:

LORD, you have searched me and known me.
You know when I sit down and when I rise up;
you discern my thoughts from far away.
You search out my path and my lying down,
and are acquainted with all my ways.

—Psalm 139:1–3

For Augustine, too, God was "more intimate to me than I am to myself," and to be found in his most lasting and real desires. But only after he peeled away the layers of fleeting or false desires could Augustine even discover a will to seek God, to heed the words of Isaiah: "Seek the Lord while he may be found, call upon him while he is near." (Isaiah 55:6)

Discernment is the practice of seeking a very near God who searches out "my path and my lying down"—and whose grace allows us to do that kind of careful searching. This is a book about selving, about finding out who you really are. It's about helping you to understand all the desires in your heart and discern which ones will point you toward a life of passion. For with discernment comes the grace to live in a way that keeps all our "goings graces," to use Hopkins's words—whether we are rich or poor, healthy or sick—without regard to what others tell us is important.

Hopkins ends his poem with a kind of promise:

I say móre: the just man justices;
Keeps grace: thát keeps all his goings graces;
Acts in God's eye what in God's eye he is—
Chríst—for Christ plays in ten thousand places,
Lovely in limbs, and lovely in eyes not his
To the Father through the features of men's faces.

What he points us toward is a way of living in which all our actions, deliberations, choices, emotions, and even suffering move us in the direction of God's promises of eternal life. "The just man justices;

/ Keeps grace" in all things. "Justice" is a biblical word for the relationships that characterize God's perfect world. It is as if Hopkins is saying that the life of discernment is a life in which we become conduits for turning a darkened world light again. In so doing, we act "in God's eye what in God's eye" we are. In Peter's second letter, he points to these promises. He writes, "He has given us, through these things, his precious and very great promises, so that through them . . . you may become participants of the divine nature." (2 Peter 1:4)

Taking a long, loving look at the real allows us to see that "Christ plays in ten thousand places." Christ plays in small villages in El Salvador, on streets torn by gang violence, in classrooms and in family homes, in hospitals and clinics, in refugee camps, in boardrooms and meeting halls, on playgrounds and fields, in scholarly texts and cookbooks, and in all imaginations of people seeking to love creatively and courageously.

The following chapters are meditations on discernment. Each is an invitation to consider how we sometimes shortchange who we are deep down and how we can live most authentically. Too often we say to ourselves: *What I do is what everyone else does.* But God's invitation is to say this: *What I do is me.*

The great philosopher Martin Buber once told the story of a rabbi named Zusya who, approaching his death, observed that in the coming life he would not be asked why he was not Moses but why he was not Zusya. Similarly, the poet Rumi wrote about how great a gift the real self is:

> If you are here unfaithfully with us,
> you're causing terrible damage.
> If you've opened your loving to God's love,
> you're helping people you don't know
> and have never seen.

To selve—to be the real self that God has created as a gift to the world—is to have faith that "you're helping people you don't know / and have never seen." It is the vigilant practice of discerning your authentic desire: the real self that God has created and invites you to cocreate through the choices you make. If your direction is toward love, which according to Dante "moves the sun and the other stars," your deepest vocation will be fulfilled.

A practical note before we begin this pilgrimage: Bring a journal with you. Throughout these pages are questions—these are stopping points along the way, reminders that every pilgrimage is not only about a destination but also about what unfolds along the path. Reflect awhile, and write down what moves in you, for that might well be the place where God is asking you to stay for a while.

1

TRAVEL THE UNPAVED ROAD

Generations have trod, have trod, have trod;
And all is seared with trade; bleared, smeared with toil;
And wears man's smudge and shares man's smell: the soil
Is bare now, nor can foot feel, being shod.
—Gerard Manley Hopkins, SJ, from "God's Grandeur"

Your passport to life has already been stamped. You have gone through customs. You are alive, and you are living in a very busy world.

The beginning of discernment is quite simply the awareness that you live in a world not of your own choosing. You are subject to its laws and affected by its social mores. You interact with people who, for the most part, are in your life for reasons that have less to do with your choices and much more to do with choices made by others over centuries. You speak their language; you are from the place where they landed. You have been thrown into the world, and now you must decide what to do here. How do you do that?

Well, you look around at what others are doing and copy them. Babies imitate their mothers. Toddlers mimic the language patterns of adults. Children watch their parents closely. Students look at what the bigger kids are doing, whether in early grades or in college. Then off to work, where you pay attention to those who are successful and copy them. If you desire holiness, you imitate Christ or the saints. You buy books from the people who have achieved success—how to

1

make money, how to lose weight, how to raise kids, how to organize your home, how to run a marathon, maybe even how to pray. (I can recommend one or two.)

On some level this pattern is unavoidable, especially when you are getting to know a new place. Imitation, or mimesis (as Aristotle called it), is a profoundly human capacity. We are at our root meaning makers, persons created to do some good in the world, who look at the data of our experience in order to interpret it in poetic or pedestrian ways. We can either follow along with the crowd, going after what they desire (or are told to desire by the arbiters of culture), or we can discern a new, creative way to live—a new adventure. As Mary Oliver wrote:

> Tell me, what is it you plan to do
> with your one wild and precious life?

So you have a life: What are you going to do with it? Will you build skyscrapers or compose operas? Will you make movies or send people to Mars? Will you become rich and famous? Will you become a head of state or win a Nobel Prize?

Let's wait a moment before we send you off on your next life's adventure and ask a rather big question. Are any of those things worth desiring? What, exactly, is the good of building skyscrapers, writing operas, making movies, sending people to Mars, becoming rich and famous, or a head of state or a Nobel Prize winner?

> *What if you do all of those things and find yourself*
> *   unhappy?*
> *What if the greatness you seek is harmful to you, to others,*
> *   to the world, or to the kingdom God is trying to build?*
> *Is God calling you to walk an unpaved road?*

RESISTING THE URGE TO COPY OTHERS

Let me introduce you to a character from Dave Eggers's novel *The Circle*, a young woman named Mae whose career path at a tech company is a parable of desires that take her away from her most authentic self. Hers is a cautionary tale about how sometimes our desires steer us to be like everyone else, and we need to have the courage to mark out a new path for our wild and precious lives.

Mae is a few years out of college, working a dead-end job, when a friend helps her get a job at the coolest company in the world. The Circle is a tech conglomerate that has bought out or overtaken Google, Facebook, Twitter, and every other Silicon Valley wannabe. Everything about the Circle is ahead of its time: the open campus with tons of recreational activities, the organic farm, the health center, the minigolf area, the movie theater, the bowling alleys, the grocery store. The ten-thousand-plus employees have free access to the on-campus dorms. In short, the Circle is like college, only they pay you to be there:

> Outside the walls of the Circle, all was noise and struggle, failure and filth. But here, all had been perfected. The best people had made the best systems and the best systems had reaped funds, unlimited funds, that made possible this, the best place to work. And it was natural that it was so, Mae thought. Who else but utopians could make utopia?

The Circle represents the summit of everything that Mae can desire. She has a job that people outside the Circle envy. She always has something interesting to do, whether it's partying with coworkers after dark, or playing kickball, or going to a brunch with people who are interested in Portugal.

The ethos of the company is built on fostering a complete circle of communication through technology. Social media, streaming real-time video all over the world, and constant awareness of one's

connection to others through phones and cameras provide employees with an almost divine knowledge of the world. Yet there are Circle skeptics, including Mae's former boyfriend Mercer, who casts a
wary eye on the creeping omniscience of the Circle. Mercer shares
his concern that social media, the allure of the digital world, and the
monetization of everything are harming authentic person-to-person
contact:

> I mean, all this stuff you're involved in, it's all gossip. It's people
> talking about each other behind their backs. That's the vast
> majority of this social media, all these reviews, all these com-
> ments. Your tools have elevated gossip, hearsay and conjecture to
> the level of valid, mainstream communication.

Mae dismisses Mercer's complaints, though, seeing only the good
that the company represents. What she sees are the limitless possibilities opened up by the Circle: people sharing instant communication, making their needs and desires known. The Circle, she
believes, will transform democracy itself when politicians "go live,"
streaming their lives in real time so their constituents can vote in an
instant on this or that idea. The scope of the Circle is total: it will
make human beings like God.

Mae and her friend Francis have a brief interaction with a former
divinity school student, a middle-aged man who gives voice to this
growing power of the Circle:

> "Now all humans will have the eyes of God. You know this pas-
> sage? 'All things are naked and opened unto the eyes of God.'
> Something like that. You know your Bible?" Seeing the blank
> looks on the faces of Mae and Francis, he scoffed and took a long
> pull from his drink. "Now we're all God. Every one of us will
> soon be able to see, and cast judgment upon, every other. We'll
> see what He sees. We'll articulate His judgment. We'll channel
> His wrath and deliver His forgiveness. On a constant and global

level. All religion has been waiting for this, when every human is a direct and immediate messenger of God's will. Do you see what I'm saying?"

Once upon a time, people ascribed anything that was unknown or mysterious to God. What the man puts his finger on in this passage is the sense that technology can replace God, making us almost omniscient. Moreover, technology can provide its own morality: the *vox populi*, the voice of the people. "We'll channel His wrath and deliver His forgiveness," the man says. Is this not what we see in the prevalence of virtual shaming and public confession? The desire to condemn others or be forgiven by the *vox populi*?

Yet what lies underneath Eggers's narrative is an uneasiness about the way that the voice of the people has replaced God. Bowing to the pressure to gain social approval may have a dark, shadow side. It may compromise our ability to discern the way our gifts might lead us to new paths and new relationships. For Mae, whose identity at the Circle is built almost entirely on the approval of others, there is a high cost of social approval: She starts to lose herself. She also begins to prioritize relationships with virtual friends and forgets about the importance of relationships with those closest to her. In going totally virtual, she loses her soul.

What if we could have digital access to everyone's innermost life?

How might we judge ourselves according to the number of likes we receive?

How might our actions change if we measured ourselves by social approval?

KEEPING UP WITH THE JONESES

When we compare ourselves to others, we lose sight of what makes us unique and begin to question whether we are good enough. And what is becoming a growing concern for many is the way that social media accelerates this process of measuring ourselves against others. According to the Pew Research Center, 92 percent of teens are online every day, and nearly a quarter report being online "almost constantly." Since adolescence is a period when much of a person's developmental work involves coming to a nuanced understanding of the relationships between self and others, it is little surprise that we see a host of concerns related to mimetic pressure: from cyberbullying to self-harming behavior facilitated by social media; from sexting and other forms of digitally facilitated sexual behavior to various forms of addiction. Mimetic pressures are real, and in the digital age, they are on steroids.

Anne Becker, a researcher at Harvard Medical School, has studied the link between media consumption and body image in young women in Fiji. The key takeaway from her 1990s study was that after the introduction of television, there was a notable rise in adolescent girls' eating disorder symptoms, connected to watching shows like *Beverly Hills, 90210* and *Melrose Place*. More recently, Becker has observed that the influence of media is not limited to those who access it directly; it extends to those who are part of social networks where digital consumption takes place. If one person is comparing herself to a TV model, then all her friends get the message that the TV model is the one whom everyone is supposed to imitate. And then they all start to feel inadequate.

The bottom line is that Becker's studies point to the power of media and social networks to misshape desire, especially among young people, who are particularly vulnerable to mimetic pressure. These networks have the power to present images of people—Photoshopped and airbrushed—as perfect objects of desire. Over time, a kind of contagion develops: Everyone wants to be like the perfect people. People's desire is directed toward a common, unattainable object, and the inability to attain it leads them to develop patterns of self-loathing. "I'm not a perfect model." "I'm not a great athlete." "I'm not a brain surgeon." These patterns of mis-shaped desire obscure much more fundamental questions that lead to growth: What are my gifts, and how might I use them to touch those around me? What does the world need from me? Who are the people in my life who need my generosity, my love, my attention?

But are young people all that different from older adults? At every stage of life there is a temptation to be a little bit better than the poor souls around us. We have an elaborate vocabulary for this rat race, from childhood to adulthood: "popular," "prestigious," "acclaimed," "well known," "famous," and so on. What's more, we race to make our groups the best, whether it's a sports team or a nation. We elevate the accomplishments of our group and assault those of another, as if happiness in life were a winner-take-all proposition. In adulthood, the race is the same but the prizes change. Bragging about being the fastest in fourth grade is not much different from driving an expensive car or chest-thumping about how great your group is. All are visible markers of being better than other people. Is that what you really desire?

Pause and consider these questions:
Do you find yourself getting caught up in competition with others?
Are your desires pulling you away from what feels right or lasting in your heart? From what God wants for you?

Let me point out the obvious: happiness and being the best don't always go hand in hand. If that were true, then we would expect that our cultural elites—athletes, movie stars, billionaires, entertainers, politicians—would all be perfectly happy. But that's not the case. Recent studies suggest exactly the opposite: being super successful may actually make one more prone to depression. Deborah Serani, a psychologist and author of the award-winning book *Living with Depression*, has worked with many cultural elites over the years. She writes:

> There's no doubt in my mind that they struggle more with depression. . . . They constantly compare themselves to the Joneses. Countries that are low-income, on the other hand, have low depression rates. When you come from [a] premier country, there's extreme competition and extreme feelings of failure: You constantly ask yourself, "Am I a *have*, or a *have-not*? Or am I an *almost-have*?"

There seems to be something fundamentally wrong with us. We are constantly comparing ourselves to others and measuring our own happiness in relation to them. When we look at those who have more than we have, we are saddened. When we look at those who have less, we become a little happier. The pattern has been studied by many over the years, and the evidence is overwhelming. Here is how the journalist Shane Snow puts it:

> So how does one avoid billionaire's depression? Or regular person's stuck-in-a-dead-end-job, lack-of-momentum-fueled depression?
>
> Harvard Business School professor Teresa Amabile took on the question in the mid-2000s in a research study of white-collar employees. She tasked 238 pencil pushers in various industries to keep daily work diaries. The workers answered open-ended questions about how they felt, what events in their days stood out. Amabile and her fellow researchers then dissected the 12,000

resulting entries, searching for patterns in what affects people's "inner" work lives the most dramatically.

The answer, it turned out, was simply *progress*. A sense of forward motion. *Regardless of how small.*

There is another word for progress, one that has the ring of a life's purpose in it—"mission." Mission is the feeling of being sent (from the Latin *missio*) to do something with your life, the nagging sensibility that you have gifts to offer the world, even if in a small corner of it. The primary task of a person thrown into the world is to discover what that mission might be, regardless of how small.

So a key question for discernment, for finding out your true desires, is this:

> *How might I become aware of mimetic pressures—that is, the pressures to do what others are doing and so to fit in? And how might I develop practices that help me not to become beholden to them?*

To ask it a little differently:

> *How can I become smart about how much I imitate others, and how can I be free to be myself?*

FIND REFLECTIVE SPACE

The prerequisite for attaining that kind of self-knowledge and freedom is to find reflective space—that is, both physical and psychological space in which we are able to let go of the usual distractions and pay attention to the teeming world that is our inner lives. We must put down our phones, turn off our screens, and reconnect with the real, living world. And when we do, we not only open ourselves to the benefits of better health and mental well-being but also afford ourselves the opportunity to know what is going on in our conscious and subconscious minds, as we strain to find expression in everyday life.

Today, there is a growing body of research that points to the relationships between our environment and our physical and mental well-being. Environmental psychologists are shedding light on the way physical space affects us: how being in a beautiful national park affects our brains in ways radically different from sitting in a cubicle, for example. Doctors are emphasizing how physical exercise can dramatically improve mental health and overall well-being. And I see a link between the environment and our inner life in the reflective essays my students have written over the years in response to an assignment to spend no less than an hour in a beautiful natural setting. They find an opening to reflect on important relationships, experiences, and desires. Environment matters: the natural world does not instant-message us, ask us to buy something, entice us to turn our attention from one thing to the next, or demand approval. It invites us to contemplate the really real.

Our bodies, our minds, and our spirits crave a connection with natural beauty. And when we give ourselves the chance to experience it—whether by going outside to breathe fresh air, hiking a mountain path, or simply walking the dog unplugged, we offer ourselves the opportunity to listen to that inner voice of desire. And with daily practice, we'll allow ourselves to return to the fundamental questions that drive the construction of our most authentic selves:

> *What do I really want?*
> *What do other people tell me I ought to want?*
> *What do advertisers tell me I ought to want?*
> *What does the economy tell me I ought to want?*
> *Will any of these things make me happy?*

This is the most fundamental dilemma of modern life: we do not know what is really worth desiring. Many of us in the human family, at least those of us in what we poorly name "the developed world," have lost touch with our origins: our flesh, our reverence for life, our dependence upon one another, our common home, our aspirations for meaning and beauty. Too often we glance nervously around for clues about what to desire, believing that the satisfaction of mimetic pressures will lead to happiness. Yet these various kinds of alienation lead us no closer to happiness; they lead us to compulsions and addictions.

I agree with the poet Marianne Moore's assessment:

satisfaction is a lowly
thing, how pure a thing is joy.

What we find in discernment are many forms of small desires that scratch at us for satisfaction. Most of them are rooted in a false sense of self and present themselves as shadows of more authentic desires. We're bored, so we watch TV or stream movies that force-feed us images of false desires. We're hungry, so we find ourselves craving whatever food is advertised on the screen we're looking at. We're lonely, so we find ourselves turned on by the glossy photos we see or movies we watch. In short, we allow digital puppeteers to manipulate us and entice us to want things that won't make us happy. Researchers who study "captology," which comes from the phrase "computers as persuasive technologies," are shedding light on how technology has dramatically refined the ways advertisers and companies entice us to click, like, gamble, and purchase our way away from our true selves. At some point, it is necessary for us to interrupt this cascade of false desires. And that interruption is as close to the real world that our senses can behold when we tear them away from distraction.

In the Gospels, Jesus uses the image of scattered seeds to tell a story about the lure of false desires. In the story, the sower spreads seeds along four kinds of ground, where some take root and some do not. On a path, birds eat up the seeds. On rocky ground, the sun's heat scorches the seed and it dies. On ground covered with thorns, the seed grows but then is choked. Finally, on good soil, the seed takes root and grows beautifully, producing enough grain to feed many people. The parable is meant to challenge Jesus' followers about the ways that daily concerns choke out the seeds that bring forth fruit in their lives. We all might start with an intention to become strong, authentic people, building our lives around relationships, good practices of self-care, awareness of others and a desire to serve, and maybe even prayer. But this "seed" of authentic desire can fall on a path of success, in which all choices are secondary to the desire to rise to the top. And so these good intentions wither and die. Similarly, we can allow the seeds of new commitments—say, the resolve to give money to the poor—to be choked by fear of financial stress or job loss. Or we may find that others' demands on us, whether at work, at home, or among friends, slowly draw us away from exploring the inner life that might otherwise grow into a new form of self-giving to the world.

Jesus' parable invites us to consider the sources of desire in our lives. Too often, he says, "the cares of the world, and the lure of wealth, and the desire for other things come in and choke the word, and it yields nothing." Developing an authentic self, he suggests, requires cultivating the ground of our inner lives, so that the seed may take root and bring forth all the virtues that lead to a great soul. That cultivation is a daily practice that, little by little, forms us into people capable of great love. We must ask ourselves:

Which of my desires are rooted in mimetic pressures—"the cares of the world, and the lure of wealth, and the desire for other things"—and which are rooted in my very self, who God has created and placed in the world?

Speaking to his disciples, Jesus is challenging them not to let anxieties get in the way of hearing the word of God, the word that speaks to them of who they really are and what they are capable of doing with God's grace. The parable is an invitation to reflection.

What are the ways in which my joy in life is crowded out by small desires?
What trials have made my heart rocky ground?
What are the thorns in my life—the cravings, the lure of wealth, or anxieties—that choke off my receiving the love of God?

Jesus points us toward a source of joy: living a life with roots sunk deep into soil teeming with life, so that all we do bursts forth beauty.

Who could say no to such a promise? The problem, though, is that we live in a world where "all is seared with trade," as Hopkins puts it in the poem at the top of this chapter. Imagine for a moment that the sower is sowing his seed through the streets of the city or town where you live. Instead of falling on rocky or thorny ground, most of the seed falls on parking lots and highways, with some perhaps falling into soil. Very little fruit would be brought forth in such a world. So, too, in such a world, manufactured cravings, which bury our authentic desires, "intrude and choke the word, and it bears no fruit."

HOW DISCERNMENT HELPS US BEAR FRUIT

Let me carry the metaphor of scattered seed just a bit further and call to mind the image of a seedling bursting forth between cracks of pavement. Life can be tenacious, sprouting anew even in a harsh environment. Hopkins writes about this reality:

And for all this, nature is never spent;
There lives the dearest freshness deep down things.

He reminds us that we are never alone in a world of false desires. Discernment can be described as the practiced art of cultivating our inner soil, so to speak: working through the layers of desires that invade that space, taking a long, loving look at the roots and branches of those desires, and electing which ones will bring forth the greatest fruit. Primarily, it is a practice of reflection, contemplation, and imagination. It involves slowing down to consider the meaning of our experiences; turning toward God in contemplation of the way that God is embedded within all our experiences, good and bad; and beginning to imagine a world in which our most authentic self might bear witness to the grandeur of God. As with any practice, discernment becomes habitual when we undertake it regularly. Its fruits spill forward into the way we become aware of our daily lives and our daily choices, for we begin to develop the habit of considering how our experiences will affect that inner soil, that readiness to receive the gifts that God gives us.

The promise of discernment is the promise of freedom. Not in the small sense of doing or getting exactly what we want—which would eventually be a kind of hell—or in the political sense of having no one tell us what to do, which can foster selfishness. Freedom in the deepest sense is becoming one's most authentic self, held back neither by societal pressures nor by false desires. It arises from a new kind of social imaginary rooted in the gospel, a gospel that proclaims glad tidings to the poor, liberty to captives, recovery of sight to the blind, and freedom to the oppressed. (Luke 4:18) That kind of social imaginary shapes the very desires that propel us toward life choices; it embeds us within a community of hope; it gives meaning to our life, keeping all our goings graces.

NEXT STEPS:

1. Plan to spend an hour in nature, either sitting and beholding a beautiful space or engaging in some type of movement (e.g., walking, biking). Bring no devices that require power, and plan for no distractions (go somewhere where you'll avoid running into people you know). Pay attention to the dynamics of your consciousness during this period. What do you experience? What are the sources of distraction? What do you notice about the pattern of your desires (even those immediate ones that tempt you to check your phone)?

2. Spend some uninterrupted time with a meditative text, perhaps Scripture, a poem, or an icon. What happens when you give your undivided attention to that text?

3. Next time you watch TV or go online, pay careful attention to the ads you see. What desires are these ads trying to elicit? What do the advertisers want you to want?

4. Consider which desires have guided your life at different stages. How is what you desire for yourself now shaped by what you see others around you desiring? In what ways are your desires authentic expressions of the kind of person God has made you to be? How are you unique, and what gifts can you offer to others?

2

SEEK GRACED
UNDERSTANDING

And the azurous hung hills are his world-wielding shoulder
Majestic—as a stallion stalwart, very-violet-sweet!—
These things, these things were here and but the beholder
Wanting; which two when they once meet,
The heart rears wings bold and bolder
And hurls for him, O half hurls earth for him off
under his feet.
—Gerard Manley Hopkins, SJ, from "Hurrahing in Harvest"

Developing the habit of discernment is fundamentally about understanding who you are, what you desire, and how to live faithfully. In
the previous chapter, we explored some obstacles to self-knowledge
that are rooted in the unhealthy desire to imitate others. In this
chapter, we'll explore another facet of self-knowledge, one that
emerges through the practice of what I describe as "graced understanding." To achieve this, we'll need to pay attention to our ordinary memories.

MEMORY AND MEANING

Recently my wife and I were cleaning out the basement, and we
came across some old pictures of our eldest daughter from when she
was an only child. There was nothing particularly interesting about

17

the pictures themselves: she is sitting in the kitchen eating birthday cake, playing with toys, putting a pie plate on her uncle's head. Most people would glance at these and then put them aside. But for us, each photo evoked a powerful and lovely memory. We delighted in the early days of parenting, hard won after many years of struggle and pain. And while it would be a stretch to describe each day during those early years as perfect, there is still something about that time that makes us revel in the memories.

You have probably had similar experiences of reminiscing. Memory can be a paradox: we can have positive feelings even as we remember difficult times, and we can look back critically on experiences that seemed fun at the time. Most often, we find, ordinary experiences transform into cherished memories, their beauty becoming more evident over time. Memory can change the meaning of our experiences.

Yet our ability to reminisce and savor these experiences can often be crowded out by more pressing demands of a busy life. I have noticed my own attention span sometimes compromised by what I call "hyperlink thinking," when I start on one topic, then recall something else, then something else, until I'm five steps away from the original topic. The technology writer Nicholas Carr points to this phenomenon in his book *The Shallows: What the Internet Is Doing to Our Brains*, suggesting that our attention spans are shortening.

The problem is not books or technology per se; the problem is in us. Recent neurobiology studies show that we are naturally attracted to novelty, whether online, in relationships, or in entertainment. But the constant craving for novelty can diminish our ability to savor the present, to take a long, loving look at the reality of the world and our place in it. And a long, loving look is more than just taking in information; it is asking what the information means and what it demands that we do. Does today's access to limitless information make us smarter or wiser or more loving? Early in the twentieth century, T. S. Eliot diagnosed the modern problem:

> The endless cycle of idea and action,
> Endless invention, endless experiment,
> Brings knowledge of motion, but not of stillness;
> Knowledge of speech, but not of silence;
> Knowledge of words, and ignorance of the Word.
> All our knowledge brings us nearer to our ignorance,
> All our ignorance brings us nearer to death,
> But nearness to death no nearer to God.
> Where is the Life we have lost in living?
> Where is the wisdom we have lost in knowledge?
> Where is the knowledge we have lost in information?

Eliot sees a modern world moving at increasing speed—and this long before the advent of the Internet—but wonders whether the impulsive embrace of novelty really serves our greatest good. His critique of the "endless cycle of idea and action" seems to suggest that our desire for novelty is rather like our desire for sugar: both provide immediate pleasure, but both tendencies can, in the long run, be harmful if not tempered by a larger sense of what is most good for us.

What if, instead of more action, what we need is more stillness? What if, instead of more speech, we need more silence? What if all of our words—whether spoken, in an article, blog post, or group message—will make more sense if understood by attending to the Word underneath all words, the Word that gives rise to language itself? Could it be that paying more attention to silence might actually make us more attentive to one another, in the way that paying attention to what we eat makes us more attentive to our health?

> *Can you be alone with only your thoughts?*
> *Can you live free of screens and wireless Internet?*
> *Can you listen to silence?*
> *What memories emerge in your consciousness when you give*
>   *yourself time to reflect?*

Eliot's poem is a critique of the mimetic pressures that we explored in chapter 1: the drive to keep racing in order to satisfy the desire to be better than those around us. There is an "endless cycle of idea and action" everywhere, whether in the workplace or at school or home. Ideas, of course, can be creative, and they can lead to inventions that serve humanity. But underneath the desire to solve the world's problems can lurk a lingering temptation: a need to be the one whom everyone praises. Eliot urges us to develop a kind of spiritual resistance to such desire by practicing stillness. "Be still, and know that I am God," wrote the psalmist too. (Psalms 46:10)

Eliot's summons recalls the story of Elijah at the mouth of a cave, where he is waiting for a sign from God:

> Now there was a great wind, so strong that it was splitting mountains and breaking rocks in pieces before the Lord, but the Lord was not in the wind; and after the wind an earthquake, but the Lord was not in the earthquake; and after the earthquake a fire, but the Lord was not in the fire; and after the fire a sound of sheer silence. When Elijah heard it, he wrapped his face in his mantle and went out and stood at the entrance of the cave.
>
> —1 Kings 19:11–13

Elijah then hears the word of God only when he is willing to attend to the silence and wait for God to speak as God himself is willing to speak. Eliot reminds us of a similar message in his poem, that a desire to bend the world to our will can obscure the word of God. "All our knowledge brings us nearer to our ignorance" because in seeking to know everything, we are bound to ignore questions about what it all means. Our hyperlink thinking gives us knowledge of cells and maybe the leaves and branches they make up, but we miss the trees, the forests, the ecosystems, the world, the cosmos, and ultimately meaning itself. We gain more and more information but lose sight of the meaning of what we know. And what knowledge we do gain does not contribute to our grasping of a living wisdom that moves the sun and the other stars.

What we really desire is graced understanding of the world: that is, a grasp of the world as it is, created and loved by God, in order to know how we are to live in it. Taking a long, loving look at the real will satisfy that desire and allow us the opportunity not only to see the world in its integrity but also to come to understand ourselves more and more over time, in order that we might understand what good we are to do.

BECOMING BEHOLDERS

How can we develop a greater capacity to see the beauty of the world and to draw meaning from our experiences? The answer is simple: by reflecting on our experiences and memories and attending mindfully to how this practice moves us to see the world in a new way. We can learn something about how this happens from Gerard Manley Hopkins, who wrote a letter to a friend about an insight he had. One day toward the end of summer, he was fishing alone in the Elwy River in Wales, enjoying a gorgeous afternoon. As he walked home, he looked up at the clouds and the hills, and his heart was lifted by the beauty around him. In that moment, the world transformed into a glimpse of God. He saw the hills as the figure of Atlas from Greek mythology—the one who carries the earth on his back. The hills had always been there, but not before this moment had he perceived how majestic they were. His key insight, as he looked around, was that it is easy to miss the beauty around us:

> And the azurous hung hills are his world-wielding shoulder
>   Majestic—as a stallion stalwart, very-violet-sweet!—
> These things, these things were here and but the beholder
>   Wanting.

The spontaneity of Hopkins's wonder is made possible by his willingness to be in the moment, to be present to the experience of the walk home after a calm afternoon fishing. He recognizes that there is beauty all around but that too often it goes unnoticed. Recalling his images from "As Kingfishers Catch Fire," we can imagine various things happening today: a bird or a dragonfly catching the sun and bursting into light, a stone falling down an old well, a bell ringing in the distance. But if no one attends to these things, their beauty is lost to the world, known only to God.

What do we allow ourselves to see? At any given moment, our field of vision is crowded with many things. We tend to see whatever is most useful to us, especially if we are busy. We see the text from a friend rather than the face of the little girl playing with her doll. We see the thing we're working on and fail to look up, where a gorgeous sunset is just outside the window. We see the pictures on our Instagram feed that show us what others see but miss how the leaves on the trees outside have darkened since last week. We read crazy stories on Facebook and lament our political mess but then rush off to the next appointment without actually having a substantial conversation with anyone.

What we need are practices that train our eyes to see what is beautiful in people, in events, and in the world itself.

How do I figure out what is worth paying attention to?

> *Is it possible that I may miss the opportunity to behold*
> *beauty because I'm too busy?*

Hopkins's experience on the way home from fishing is a reminder that our busyness can keep us from experiencing the majesty of God. For what happens in gazing and beholding is an awareness that the veil between God and ourselves is entirely of our own making, and that we might pull it aside in order to know the source of our freedom and joy:

The heart rears wings bold and bolder
And hurls for him, O half hurls earth for him off under his feet.

Notice that we are not talking about having extraordinary experiences, like climbing Mount Everest or winning the Nobel Prize. Rather, we are talking about having ordinary vision that allows us to see things anew, such that "the heart rears wings." There is beauty to be found in the everyday. Jesus, when speaking in parables, describes people as having eyes that don't see and ears that don't hear (see Matthew 13:15 and Mark 8:18).

> *What gets in the way of my beholding?*
> *What am I choosing to see instead of the beauty right in*
> *front of me, whether in nature, or the face of another*
> *person, or a city street, or a workplace, or the*
> *grocery store?*
> *What am I looking for when I see the world?*

All of us are vulnerable to various forms of bias, ways of seeing the world that limit our understanding. We are on the way to work or school and don't see the tender way the mother is helping her child onto the school bus. We are in the store, hunting for items we need, and fail to see the people who work there, as well as their need to be treated like human beings. We watch movies or TV shows and don't ask how the money we spend on them will be used. Our vision is limited, because so often we are looking only at ourselves and our small circle of people. Part of our bias is rooted in mimesis—our culture teaches us what is worth desiring, and it can be difficult to gain the critical perspective to challenge what others tell us is good. How do we learn what is really worth desiring?

GRACED UNDERSTANDING

Seeking graced understanding means developing practices and habits that help us take a step back from our day-to-day lives and allow God to speak to us as a friend who shows us what it all means. Socrates once opined that the unexamined life is not worth living and that what makes life meaningful is the cultivated practice of loving wisdom. His foundational insight, which many over the ages have built upon, is at the heart of graced understanding. What we need is enough distance from the flow of our daily activities that we have the opportunity to pursue that understanding. Fortunately, we do not need to retreat into a monastery every day; we can retreat into the memory of our experiences through a practice that has been known for centuries as the Examen. Simply put, the Examen is a prayer developed by St. Ignatius that involves taking ten minutes each day to come to a deeper, graced understanding of one's experience and God's place in it. More than just remembering the past day, the Examen is an attempt to discern who we are as a person who has just had these experiences. Every experience involves not only what's "out there," the people and things that I interact with, but also what's "in here," in me, affecting me even as I affect the world around me.

George Aschenbrenner, SJ, describes this practice in a seminal 1972 essay:

> The examen is not simply a matter of the natural power of our memory and analysis going back over a part of the day. It is a matter of Spirit-guided insight into our life and courageously responsive sensitivity to God's call in our heart. What we are seeking here is that gradually growing appreciative insight into *the mystery that I am* [Emphasis added].

What Aschenbrenner puts his finger on is the complexity of our inner lives and the need to be attentive to the ways that God can guide our memory toward graced understanding through the practice of the Examen. In other words, by paying attention to our inner lives, we might discover that we are confused, overwhelmed, misled, silenced, doubtful, or afraid. Our real selves might be hidden behind fear or hurt, silenced because of societal pressures, suppressed because of unhealthy desires. I may lose touch with my authentic self, wearing a mask that enables me to get through daily life but that slowly makes me unable to know myself—"the mystery that I am"—whom God has created to do a unique good in the world. Practicing the Examen, Aschenbrenner suggests, allows us to name where we are and come to a greater understanding of how we might achieve greater freedom.

Alternatively, there may be experiences that allow me to selve, to be myself and proclaim myself to the world. There may be moments when I feel a new freedom to be myself, a new sense of appreciation for God's gifts to me, a new sense of the world's possibilities and my abilities to make the world better. I might spontaneously feel myself falling in love and seeing the world in a transformed way. The Examen can help me celebrate and give thanks for those experiences by going back to them and inhabiting them. Perhaps it was a test or a project that, in retrospect, I discover that I did really well on, or an interaction with a friend or loved one that helped me come to a new insight about myself. It is good to return to such graces and ask what they tell me about myself, my priorities, and my hopes.

What can make these experiences of darkness (which St. Ignatius called desolation) or light (consolation) difficult to discern are the confusing messages of past experiences. Perhaps we now think of the flush of first falling in love as naive, or we remember the initial resistance we felt toward something that we now feel thankful for. The way we remember, understand, and value past experiences can change in light of new experiences, making our lives feel like a platform made of shifting sand. How can we discern and make sense of these experiences authentically? How can we come to some certainty about the kind of person God calls us to be?

A friend of mine recently related the experience of moving to a new city. He was totally resistant to the idea, having lived in the same area his whole life. His wife was urging a move, though, largely because the new city had a great school for their son with special needs. The idea of moving caused a good deal of friction between them, but my friend eventually consented. Several months later, he humbly related that the move was one of the best decisions of his life. What he had experienced as a source of stress was transformed in his memory into a kind of graced understanding. The move was an act of sacrificial love: he gave up his own desire to live in a place he knew and loved in order to pursue good for his wife and son. But over time he came to understand how good the move was for himself, as well.

In seeking graced understanding, we are doing more than checking off memories from the past day. We are trying to see our experiences as God sees them, transforming them in our memory through a kind of love that we often do not fully apply to ourselves. We are trying to become aware of God's presence, even when we are unaware of him or antagonistic toward him. The prayer of St. Ignatius of Loyola, known as the Suscipe, expresses this desire:

> Take, Lord, and receive all my liberty, my memory, my understanding, and all my will—all that I have and possess. You, Lord, have given all that to me. I now give it back to you, O Lord. All of it is yours. Dispose of it according to your will. Give me your love and your grace, for that is enough for me.

Through a series of five steps, the Examen helps your real self, sometimes buried beneath layers of false desires, grow in friendship with God. It is a prayer for freedom, that is, for a life that shows the person God has created you to be. By placing your liberty in God's hands, you let go of the false freedoms hawked by advertisers, bureaucrats, and entertainers. By offering God your memory, you are asking God to transform your experiences—good and bad—into something beautiful. By giving God your understanding, you relinquish the control that might tempt you to use people and things to your own ends, allowing God to steer you toward a greater end than you could ever imagine. And ultimately, in handing your will over to God, you make the prayer Mary made in response to the angel your own: "Let it be done to me according to your word."

FIVE STEPS OF THE EXAMEN

The Examen is a pause in your day long enough to converse with God, so that "heart speaks to heart." This phrase comes from the writings of St. Francis de Sales, who describes the nature of prayer as an intimate conversation between lovers:

> Truly the chief exercise in mystical theology is to speak to God and to hear God speak in the bottom of the heart; and because this discourse passes in most secret aspirations and inspirations, we term it a silent conversing. Eyes speak to eyes, and heart to

heart, and none understand what passes save the sacred lovers who speak.

Far from a formula that must be recited, the five steps of the Examen represent directions in a conversation between intimate friends. These steps become natural after some practice, since they are designed to help us come to a shared understanding of how we have experienced the past day and how we hope to enter meaningfully into the next day.

STEP 1: LIGHT

The first step is to ask for the grace of light that might come from seeing ourselves the way God does. Our prayer is the prayer of Solomon, asking God for a heart and mind that are (as different translations have it) "listening," "discerning," and "understanding." The book of Proverbs expresses this desire well:

> My child, if you accept my words
> and treasure up my commandments within you,
> making your ear attentive to wisdom
> and inclining your heart to understanding;
> if you indeed cry out for insight,
> and raise your voice for understanding;
> if you seek it like silver,
> and search for it as for hidden treasures—
> then you will understand the fear of the Lord
> and find the knowledge of God.
> For the Lord gives wisdom;
> from his mouth come knowledge and understanding.
>
> —Proverbs 2:1–6

As you enter into a conversation with the God who knows you more intimately than you know yourself (Psalm 139), pray that God might grant you the wisdom to remember your experiences with graced understanding.

STEP 2: GRATITUDE

The second step in your conversation with God is to express gratitude, giving thanks for the people and things that you have experienced over the past day, especially those that might have escaped your notice. Maybe you will recall a kind word or look from a stranger; maybe you will take a moment to savor the goodness of a friendship; maybe you will attend to how grateful you are for the place where you live. At times, this step will be as natural as breathing—when life is going well, it's easy for our hearts to cry out to God spontaneously with thanksgiving. Yet it is also beneficial to practice gratitude when our hearts do not feel it so easily. During hard times, it can be freeing to hunt for things to give thanks for, no matter how small. To use an ancient image, a heart full of gratitude is like a jar filled with honey—there is no room in it for vinegar. Contemporary studies of happiness also point to gratitude as a key factor. Robert Emmons and his colleagues from the Greater Good Science Center at the University of California, Berkeley, have studied gratitude in people of all ages and point to a number of benefits from practices like keeping gratitude journals for even a short time. They've discovered that people who regularly practice gratitude show these benefits:

PHYSICAL

- Stronger immune systems
- Fewer aches and pains
- Lower blood pressure
- Increased exercise and better self-care
- Longer periods of sleep and increased refreshment upon waking

PSYCHOLOGICAL

- Higher levels of positive emotions
- More alert, alive, and awake
- More joy and pleasure
- More optimism and happiness

SOCIAL

- More helpful, generous, and compassionate
- More forgiving
- More outgoing
- Less lonely and isolated

What's important to note is that we are not talking about starting with a *feeling* of gratitude; we are talking about *practicing* gratitude regardless of how we feel at the time. One of the key lessons I've learned as a spiritual director and as a parent is that feelings are a rather terrible compass for making decisions. Too often they are immediate responses to stimuli and don't allow easy entry to the depths of our consciousness or our unconscious lives. Feelings are like waves on the ocean's surface—they don't reveal the deep and powerful currents underneath. Practicing gratitude over time allows us to access the depths of our inner lives so we can more easily converse with God.

STEP 3: REVIEW

The third step is a review of the day. In this step, we deliberately try to reconstruct our experiences so we can see them through the light of friendship with God. It's similar to the way our perception of a movie or TV show changes when we're watching it with another person. We begin to see it through their eyes and are less likely to be limited by our own biases. Note that this review involves more than allowing immediate memories to bubble up to the surface of our consciousness. Too often we fixate on those experiences that caused the most visceral reaction. Maybe it was someone who cut us off in traffic, raising our anger. Maybe it was what we said to a coworker that we now regret. Strong emotions tend to leave the strongest impressions on our memories. What we aim for in the review of our day is a patient, measured walk through our experience, with God at our side. We allow God room to point out elements of our day that we might have otherwise passed over.

It can be good to start in chronological order from where you were twenty-four hours ago. Walk through your memories, asking questions like these:

What was I feeling when I experienced these things?
Who are the people who touched me?
What experiences left the strongest emotional impressions on me, positive or negative?
Where did I sense consolation? Desolation?
When did I most feel myself? When did I feel I had to pretend to be someone else?
When did I spontaneously feel gratitude? Resentment? Hopefulness? Fear? Anger? Other emotions?

Author Dennis Hamm, SJ, uses the image of rummaging to describe what happens when you review your day. Rummaging suggests that we not just look at the most obvious things but that we dig deeper in order to assess whether less obvious things have value. It may well be that God wants to draw us into conversation by remembering one small act of kindness we've received. Perhaps that small act is even more important than grand accomplishments.

STEP 4: CONVERSATION

The fourth step is a conversation with God about one such element of the past day. In talking to God, we are looking to understand what that experience might mean for the deeper currents of our life: what we hope for, what we fear, what we find most meaningful or holy. If, during this movement, we find that we desire forgiveness, we ask God to forgive. If we are rejoicing, we invite God to rejoice with us. If we are scared, we bring that fear before God and ask for God's comfort, reminding ourselves that one of Jesus' most common sayings was some version of "Don't be afraid."

During this step, we seek what the etymology of the word "conversation" suggests: a "turning with" God, a dwelling with God (the word comes from the Latin *convertere*, "to turn around"). An image I find helpful is the way that athletes or performers will sometimes go over video of their performances with coaches or directors, trying to understand both what went well and what needs improvement. Similarly, we are asking God to show us not only how our life reveals the beauty of God's gifts but also the ways in which we have yet to realize the beauty that God desires to bring forth in us.

STEP 5: HOPE

The fifth step is about hope for the future. We look with God to the coming day and allow God's grace to help us face whatever experiences will unfold, from the most mundane to the most challenging. Psalm 23 articulates this hope well: "I fear no evil; for you are with me," and "goodness and mercy shall follow me all the days of my life." I recall that God has created me to do some good in the world and that if I am willing to listen to the way God steers me toward that goodness—however unlikely or unexpected—I will find my joy.

With practice, these five steps become as natural as any conversation with a friend. And over time, the Examen will help us build graced understanding, so that this loving look at our past experience also becomes a loving look at our present experience. God's grace spills over into your everyday life, and you will begin to seek out ways to act with grace. *That* helps you become more and more the realest version of yourself.

NEXT STEPS:

1. Before you begin the Examen, find a designated prayer space. You can pray the Examen anywhere—on a plane, at work, in line at the grocery store—but it may be helpful to choose a peaceful, quiet place at home where you can always go to pray.

2. To help you settle and relax, light a candle or turn on some music.

3. Take a few deep breaths. Feel your body begin to soften and loosen.

4. Acknowledge passing thoughts and let them go. Keep breathing, and begin to feel the loving presence of God. Thoughts may distract, but try to bring yourself back to the present, with God.

5. Begin the Examen! You can try the steps outlined here, or, for a more customized experience, try Mark Thibodeaux, SJ's Reimagining the Examen app, which allows you to tailor your prayer experience based on your mood.

3

LIVE A ~~HAPPY~~ MISSIONED LIFE

There lives the dearest freshness deep down things.
—Gerard Manley Hopkins, SJ, from "God's Grandeur"

Over the past few years, I've seen more and more books on the best-seller list about how to live a happy life. Driven by advances in positive psychology, as well as thoughtful commentaries by philosophers, theologians, economists, life coaches, leadership experts, and neuroscientists, many approaches try to help people eliminate toxic habits or thought patterns and develop practices that contribute to happiness. Who wouldn't want that?

The pursuit of happiness is not a new goal—ancient philosophers such as Plato, Aristotle, Confucius, and the Buddha all proposed ways to lead a happy life. Aristotle describes happiness particularly well in his opening lines of *Nicomachean Ethics*: "Every art and every inquiry, and similarly every action and pursuit, is thought to aim at some good." But he goes on to ask what people mean by happiness. For if people knew what happiness is, it would be a lot easier to go after it. The seventeenth-century French mathematician and philosopher Blaise Pascal puts it even more forcefully:

> All men seek happiness. This is without exception. Whatever different means they employ, they all tend to this end. The cause of some going to war, and of others avoiding it, is the same desire in

both, attended with different views. The will never takes the least step but to this object. This is the motive of every action of every man, even of those who hang themselves.

Everyone wants happiness, but there is great disagreement on what it is and how we should pursue it. And with so much advice out there, how do we decide how to discern good choices in order to live an authentic life?

What we learn from practices like the Examen, described in the previous chapter, is that our lives are a combination of elements that we can control and elements that we cannot. Over time, these practices calibrate the inner compass of our lives so that we become more adept at steering ourselves toward meaning—toward God and toward the mission for which God has given us life.

What we seek, I think, is not just happiness, for too often that word suggests an emotional state that reflects our response to whether external factors are positive. Rather than focus on happiness as that state created by some object we go after, I think it is more helpful to focus on ourselves as subjects who do various things in order to find happiness. Happiness seeking is partly about what we seek, but it is also about the person who does the seeking. It is about having a worthy goal: some greater good in which we ourselves take part.

But there's a danger here: we can get too caught up in ourselves, falling into narcissistic tendencies. Some of the literature on happiness troubles me because it focuses too strongly on the self. Rather than try to distill my concerns into one sound bite, let me point them out with some questions:

> *Can we seek happiness on our own or do we need others?*
> *Is happiness something we can find with the right attitude*
>   *or skills?*

Is happiness dependent on finding the right relationships?

Is happiness only for those who have enough social capital to find the right mix of work and play?

Can poor people be happy?

How can someone be happy after tragedy?

Is happiness dependent on avoiding suffering?

Are people unhappy if they choose to live in solidarity with those who suffer?

Should we seek happiness for its own sake or for the sake of some greater good?

Many people believe in what I'd call a kind of Facebook happiness—that is, a belief that having a string of interesting life events constitutes a happy life. The major problem with Facebook happiness is that it's all about having great experiences, so if you stop having them, you're no longer happy. Life is too complicated for that model: we get sick, we go through times of doubt, we experience suffering, we encounter tragedies. At its worst, Facebook happiness can make us narcissists ignorant of others' suffering, always looking to consume the next good time.

I want to offer a different model of happiness, one that has a long pedigree. Happiness is rooted in self-possession: an awareness of who you are and the possession of the fundamental faith that your life has meaning regardless of your present circumstances. In other words, this model involves awareness of life as a kind of voyage with highs and lows, consolation and desolation, calms and storms that we navigate with an eye toward the good we can do. It is less about adapting to every changing wind and more about learning to tack when wind comes so that we may stay on course. I find this model much more attentive to the realities of life, both positive and negative, for it is rooted in a basic understanding that our experiences include both things we choose for ourselves and things over which we have no control.

Since ancient times, generations have wrestled with this question of what we have control over and what we don't. From Mesopotamia to ancient Greece and India, we find stories about the interactions between gods and mortals, stories about the complex interplay between fate and free will. In one well-known story, Sophocles describes Oedipus, who is fated to kill his father and marry his mother and whose unfortunate life unfolds that way in spite of his parents' and his own attempts to avoid that fate. In a similar vein, the Talmud has the story of Death speaking to King Solomon, telling him that two of his servants are to die. To protect them, Solomon sends them to the city of Luz, a legendary city where no one dies. But he learns from Death the next day that he had sent them to the very place where Death was to meet the servants. Stories like these can seem to suggest that life is ultimately a game ruled by fate.

Much of the most ancient biblical literature wrestles with this idea: the relationship between human freedom and the hard realities of a world in which there is suffering. Nowhere is this sentiment more poignantly expressed than by the author of Ecclesiastes 1:2–3: "Vanity of vanities! All is vanity. What do people gain from all the toil at which they toil under the sun?" In other places, the biblical texts raise similar questions of whether it is possible to have a happy life, with much of it falling into the genre called lamentation, a literary form characterized by crying out to God over the unfairness of the world. Still other texts implore God to smash enemies and give vengeance to those who have been wronged. Consider Psalm 109, which implores God to appoint an accuser (Hebrew *satan*) against the wicked: "Appoint a wicked man against him; let an accuser stand on his right. When he is tried, let him be found guilty; let his prayer be counted as sin." (6–7) The psalmist yearns for justice because the wicked one has stolen happiness from him.

Yet elsewhere, both in Scripture and in other ancient texts, there is a strong illustration of how human beings are given the power to choose a life that God or the gods demands. At the end of the Israelites' exodus from Egypt, just before they are to cross the Jordan River into the Promised Land, God speaks to the people and exhorts them to choose how they will live:

> I call heaven and earth to witness against you today that I have set before you life and death, blessings and curses. Choose life so that you and your descendants may live, loving the Lord your God, obeying him, and holding fast to him.
> —Deuteronomy 30:19–20

The author of Deuteronomy points to a fundamental truth: we experience the world as free beings. To be sure, that freedom is not absolute—we don't choose when or where to be born, whom our parents are, what language we learn, and so on. Yet we do exercise a great deal of freedom both existentially and experientially. We can choose how to react to experiences; we can make many choices over the course of a day about what to do, where to go, and how to interact with others. Ours is a "conditioned" freedom, meaning that given the limitations we experience in our lives, we nevertheless exercise free choice within those limitations. How, then, are we to discern that freedom to find meaning in our lives? To discover a purpose toward which we choose to build our life choices? To stretch ourselves in service to others, growing our hearts in such ways that, by the end of our lives, we may look in the rearview mirror and discover our happiness?

LESSONS FROM VIKTOR FRANKL

Viktor Frankl (1905–1997) was an Austrian neurologist, psychiatrist, and Holocaust survivor who received twenty-nine honorary degrees. The American Psychiatric Association honored him with the Oskar Pfister Award, which recognizes lifetime contributions in psychiatry and religion. Frankl's book *Man's Search for Meaning*, originally published in 1946, has been translated (as of this writing) into twenty-four languages and has sold more than twelve million copies worldwide. In 1991, the Library of Congress asked readers to name a book that made a difference in people's lives, and *Man's Search for Meaning* was listed as one of the ten most influential books in the United States.

Frankl's book is a memoir about his experiences in a Nazi concentration camp, focusing on how human beings can live in the face of such grotesque suffering. A second section describes the psychoanalytic theory that Frankl had begun to develop before the war but that he came to understand deeply because of his experience in the camp. Logotherapy (from the Greek, translated as "meaning healing"), as he called it, was the practice of encouraging people to reflect on what gave their lives meaning. A 1984 postscript, "The Case for a Tragic Optimism," focuses on how people might retain a "why" for living in the face of pain, guilt, and death.

What makes the book—and Frankl himself—so important is that Frankl invites us to consider the "why" of our lives, especially when we do not have the freedom to choose our circumstances. Faced with near-complete deprivation in Auschwitz, Frankl was forced to starkly confront the question of why he wanted to live. He saw around him human beings who had given up all hope on life and died. He had to turn inward and find what enabled him to keep living. And what he found was expressed simply in the language of the philosopher Friedrich Nietzsche: "He who has a why to live can bear with almost any how." In other words, Frankl learned that discovering one's meaning in life allows one to persevere even in the face of suffering. In his own case, the thought of reuniting with his wife, and later of publishing the manuscript of his book, enabled him to face the deprivations and humiliations of camp life. These goals provided him with compass points by which he could steer his life.

Frankl describes an occasion when a fellow prisoner asked him to talk about not losing hope. Many had died, some by suicide, because they had given up on life. Frankl writes of what he said to the other prisoners:

> I said that someone looks down on each of us in difficult hours—a friend, a wife, somebody alive or dead, or a God—and he would not expect us to disappoint him. He would hope to find us suffering proudly—not miserably—knowing how to die.

The important point to underscore here is that Frankl is suggesting that the source of meaning transcends the isolated self: we must look outward to find another *for whom our life is meaningful.* Elsewhere, he crafts a poignant statement on what gives life meaning, thinking about his dear wife:

> A thought transfixed me: for the first time in my life I saw the truth as it is set into song by so many poets, proclaimed as the final wisdom by so many thinkers. The truth—that love is the ultimate and the highest goal to which man can aspire. Then I grasped the meaning of the greatest secret that human poetry and human thought and belief have to impart: *The salvation of man is through love and in love.*

His use of the word "salvation" here is not merely rhetorical; he found that love saved his life in the concentration camp, because love for his wife, and the accompanying hope that he would see her again (even though he did not) kept him going. For Frankl, love is a self-transcending capacity of the human heart that gives meaning to life.

> *One who has a why to live for can bear with almost any how. What is, for you, the "why" to live? What do you live for? Whom do you live for?*

FINDING MEANING

If Frankl is right—and I deeply believe that he is—then the perfection of love is the one thing worth dedicating one's life to. But here again we confront a key question: What (or who) is worth loving? How, in other words, do we love in a way that will bring meaning? And will finding that meaning ultimately make us happy? Frankl reminds us that happiness is not an object in itself; it must emerge from a meaningful object:

> To the European, it is a characteristic of the American culture that, again and again, one is commanded and ordered to "be happy." But happiness cannot be pursued; it must ensue. One must have a reason to "be happy." Once the reason is found, however, one becomes happy automatically.

Happiness, in other words, is a by-product of a meaningful life; it emerges from a life lived in love. It is exactly the opposite of what might be called "consumer happiness"—that is, a model of happiness that arises from acquiring various objects of passing desire. Consumer happiness goes by many names and euphemisms, but they all share the common feature of positing that one can be happy by consuming something: retail therapy (shopping as a form of happiness); hookup culture (sexual overconsumption); adrenaline rush (always seeking the next thrill); getting high (seeking an altered mental state); scoring tickets (to a game, a concert, or some other event); keeping up with the Joneses (achieving social status through wealth).

All these things—and others, to be sure—may in fact yield feelings that a person can enjoy for a while. But none of them can offer happiness, since all are temporary. And some—like getting high—can be destructive over the long haul. What is problematic about all these forms of consumer happiness is that they locate happiness in *getting something*. Frankl suggests that happiness can't be pursued; it can only ensue. That is, it can arise only as something one discovers in the midst of a life lived in love. And love, if we follow St. Paul, is never selfish:

> Love is patient; love is kind; love is not envious or boastful or arrogant or rude. It does not insist on its own way; it is not irritable or resentful; it does not rejoice in wrongdoing, but rejoices in the truth. It bears all things, believes all things, hopes all things, endures all things.
>
> —1 Corinthians 13:4–7

Real love draws a person out of him- or herself. It is the exact opposite of consumer happiness (of which my earlier description of Facebook happiness is a variety, as one consumes different experiences). It is, to use an ancient Greek expression, "ecstatic"—one goes out of oneself (*ekstasis*) in love toward another.

Our model for this form of happiness is St. Ignatius of Loyola, whose experience of conversion exemplifies the relationship among discernment, mission, and happiness. Young Iñigo, as he was called, was very much a product of early sixteenth-century Spain. Like his peers, he absorbed the lifestyle and expectations of his culture. If he were alive today, he would surely excel in school and sports, go to a prestigious college, and get a lucrative job, much like Mae, who we met in chapter 1. In his day, the pattern was to follow the customs of courtly behavior, seek military glory, then achieve a position in the court of the king. He went after all of these experiences that his culture told him were valuable, and because of his type A personality, he sought to outdo those around him. The turning point was a battle against the French at Pamplona, a hopeless fight that he nevertheless entered with zeal. A cannonball shattered his leg, and he might have died had not the French treated him with compassion, and he returned home for a long convalescence. That period proved transformative.

Iñigo was restless, having exhausted his capacity to inhale new experiences that satisfied his desires. He was feeling the sixteenth-century version of what might be described as the shadow side of consumer happiness: the withdrawal that can happen when one is no longer having experiences that quench that unending thirst for false happiness. Iñigo was laid up in bed with a shattered leg and a shattered heart, for it began to dawn on him that he was doomed to be regarded as a cripple for the rest of his life. The object of his desire—glory and fame—was snatched from him. Only later, after much suffering, was he able to discern that these had been false desires and that the suffering that came from their removal was, to put it in modern-day terms, like the withdrawal that precedes one's liberation from addiction.

That liberation took time. Like anyone who faces withdrawal, Iñigo sought distraction. We might bury ourselves in our playlists or gorge on entire seasons of a streamed show. For Iñigo, though, the only recourse was reading. Worse, the only reading material he had at hand was not the swashbuckling tales of knights he had enjoyed in his youth but two books on the life of Christ and stories about the saints. But because he was desperate, he began reading.

Iñigo found himself, to his surprise, drawn to the stories. Every now and then he would daydream, having little else to do, and his mind would wander back to the stories of knights pledging themselves in service to a certain lady. At other times, though, his mind would drift back to the stories of Christ and the saints, and he noted the beginnings of a change in the pattern of the individuals he felt drawn to imitate. Iñigo began imagining himself in comparison not to the knights but to people like St. Francis of Assisi. And he found that this movement was working on his emotions and even changing the way he thought about himself. Here's how he describes what was going on inside of him (using the third person):

> When he was thinking of those things of the world he took much delight in them, but afterwards, when he was tired and put them aside, he found himself dry and dissatisfied. But when he thought of going to Jerusalem barefoot, and of eating nothing but plain vegetables and of practicing all the other rigors that he saw in the saints, not only was he consoled when he had these thoughts, but even after putting them aside he remained satisfied and joyful.
>
> Little by little he came to recognize the difference between the spirits that were stirring, one from the devil, the other from God.

Iñigo dictated these experiences to a secretary many years later—thereby giving us the text of his *Autobiography*. That secretary, Luis Gonçalves da Câmara, made a note to readers that this experience was the beginning of Iñigo's understanding of "discernment of spirits," which he developed more fully in his work *The Spiritual Exercises*. Put most simply, discernment of spirits is the careful sifting through of experiences in order to weigh which ones are rooted in more lasting desires and which are rooted in more fleeting desires. Finding God, Ignatius discovered, was about paying careful attention to his own most lasting and true desires, which ignited in him a life's mission, and about being willing to let go of those that turned him in on himself. That new path of discerning how to live a missioned life, he found, was a discovery of a new and lasting kind of happiness.

DISCERNMENT OF SPIRITS

In short, Ignatius found that attending to his inner life—his con-sciousness—was the beginning of real self-knowledge. But this can be difficult to do. Our inner life—the cauldron of swirling images, memories, feelings, compulsions, fears, hopes, and desires—can be chaotic. Psychologists, pastors, neurologists, sociologists, philoso-phers, doctors, and theologians have different perspectives on how to approach the question of what is going on inside of us. But I bet none of them would use the word "simple" to describe it. Human beings are complex; we have many things vying for our attention at any given moment. Consider the various levels of complexity that affect our self-consciousness and our consciousness of the world:

- Neurochemists, neurobiologists, and neuropsychologists are coming to a greater understanding of chemicals such as dopamine, serotonin, and others that have an impact on our mood, and they are pointing to behaviors like exercise or con-versations with friends that can significantly influence our moods.

- Psychologists who study the machinery of memory have found that strong emotional experiences often impress themselves in our memories but can also involve false memories.

- Environmental factors can impinge upon our experience of the world: heat or cold, light or dark, and the change of seasons can affect our moods.

- Internal factors can also impinge upon our experience of the world: Hunger, thirst, sexual desires, and sleep can affect our consciousness. Moreover, these internal factors can be affected by damage to the brain. To use one example, damage to the hypothalamus can induce a person to overeat and become obese.

- Experiences of violence can affect the way people treat others. Those who were abused as children, for example, are more likely to abuse others later in life.

- Human beings are liable to follow various forms of "herd mentality," mimicking the patterns of those they see around them rather than thinking freely.

This is but a small sample of the factors that affect us, often without our consent or awareness. What Ignatius intuited five centuries ago, and what many today seek to overcome, is the sense that we are not always fully in control of our very selves. Like other ancient writers who pondered the nature of happiness, Ignatius came to understand that the point is less about exercising total control over the world and more about learning to exercise greater control over ourselves.

Interestingly, Ignatius's prescription for coming to greater self-awareness and freedom is one with which many scientists and philosophers today would agree: regular practices of reflection and discernment like the Examen (described in the previous chapter) become habitual over time. I find the contemporary mindfulness movement, for example, an interesting twist on an old theme. Rooted in practices of Buddhist meditation, it involves various habits that cultivate awareness of the present moment, like meditating on one's breathing or on the various sensations (e.g., touch, smell, taste) that, say, touching and eating a raisin might evoke. Mindfulness has become all the rage at companies in Silicon Valley, for example, because of its many benefits to health and productivity. Stripped of religious language, the movement nevertheless is rooted in the recognition that spiritual practices can enhance self-understanding and pursuit of a good life. Such practices reflect a basic truth: we are often caught up in stresses and various stimuli that throw us off-kilter, causing us to crave balance.

What St. Ignatius realized was that even in the midst of the stressors of life, it is possible to discern a sense of direction and meaning by developing practices of attentiveness. The point, he came to understand, was not to remove the causes of stress. Rather, reflecting on his early experience of being drawn to imitate St. Francis and others, St. Ignatius sought to distinguish the desires that brought lasting happiness from those that brought temporary happiness followed by desolation. For him, meaning in life was not about seeking some vague form of happiness; it was about having a mission. Discernment of spirits was about coming to understand that mission. And spiritual practices were about enhancing one's conversation with God by eliminating distractions and focusing on how one can understand one's deepest, most authentic self—created by God to do some good in the world. In a word, "discernment" means practicing regular prayer.

THE MISSIONED LIFE

Developing self-knowledge through practices of reflection like the Examen is an important dimension of finding and living your life's mission. Such practices can help us interrupt unhealthy patterns of mimesis, much as Ignatius was forced to do during his convalescence. Yet self-knowledge itself is not enough. Initially, coming to a critical view of the patterns of life we've absorbed from the culture around us can feel like a void: we know what we no longer want to desire, but we might not yet have a clear-cut sense of what is worth desiring.

Again, Ignatius's life is helpful to consider. After he had distanced himself from what others around him said was valuable, he was depressed and aimless. He had a strong desire to serve God and to follow Jesus closely, but he didn't know how. Having let go of the desire to imitate knights, he chose to imitate St. Francis instead by going on a pilgrimage to Jerusalem. So he went, not exactly sure what he would do there but knowing that he wanted to do it with a clean heart. He begged his way onto a ship and eventually made it to the Holy Land, only to find that the leaders of the church there had no place for him. He returned home, dejected and unsure of how to proceed.

It would be several sometimes-frustrating years before Ignatius understood the way God was working on his consciousness. He had to swallow his pride and go back to school, begging his way through remedial grammar in order to get to the university. All the while, he preached about the life of faith and nourished a deep desire to follow wherever Jesus would take him. It was during his university years that his desires began to coalesce around a mission: specifically, in his relationship with roommates and friends, whom he instructed in the same spiritual exercises that had been so transformative in his own life. What he and his small band of friends (including St. Francis Xavier and St. Peter Faber) came to realize was that God was calling them to form a new group, which they would name the "companions of Jesus," helping souls in whatever way they could. In time, their small band—later called the Jesuits—grew and became renowned for their teaching, research, and missionary work.

If Ignatius's life is any indicator, a life of mission is not always obvious and easy. Coming to name the deep desires that give one's life meaning is only the first step in developing a missioned life. But it takes time, patience, and perseverance to listen to God over time. Even Jesus' disciples were often confused about how to be part of his mission. Peter, the leader of the disciples, got a stern rebuke from Jesus for not thinking about his mission the way God would (see Matthew 16:23). But who can blame him? All of us are limited in the way we think about our lives, formed as we are with the cultural vocabulary we absorb from our upbringing.

But if there is one lesson that becomes clear when we look at the story of Jesus and of the countless saints—not to mention men and women today whose desires lead them to lives of great generosity—it is that a life mission begins with a desire to love authentically and truly. And this mission always blossoms in beauty, regardless of how great or small its fruits. At first, it may be about learning small ways to practice generosity and compassion. But as our desire to listen to God grows, so too do our creativity and resolve in taking on new ideas and ways of serving the world God has made. Over time, we find, the practice of the missioned life moves us in the direction of great desires rooted in the love of God, blossoming in beauty, truth, and goodness—especially among those who need it most.

WHEN IN A DARK PLACE

Of course, a missioned life is not always a perfect life. Life is not only ups and no downs. Every life—whether the object of social-media envy or whether lived in perfect imitation of Jesus and the saints—will involve times of darkness. The word "desolation" (perhaps from the Latin for "without the sun") is used to describe these periods, providing a metaphor for our inner life that can spill over into the ways we live, work, and connect with others. During times of desolation, it is as if a shadow is cast over everything we do: we internalize negative messages about ourselves, we feel unworthy of the love of others, we feel worthless in our work or activities, we have a general sense of apathy or even hopelessness toward life.

Desolation is not the same as depression. The former is a spiritual condition that reflects primarily on your relationship with God and the meaning you look for in life. The latter is a medical condition, one we are coming to understand little by little. To be sure, some people have experiences when medical intervention may be necessary, and it is important to speak to a therapist. These may originate in health issues, relationship issues, job loss, or other traumas. Other times, though, we may encounter not so much a medical issue as a spiritual and psychological one: we may reflect on the ways our lives get "stuck" as a result of unwanted impasses in work, relationships, or an understanding of ourselves in the world. In such times, there are ways forward: ways to regain freedom and discern a path toward a renewed consolation.

When in a dark place, counsels Ignatius, it is important not to change anything about the way you go about your life and enter into prayer. Most important, don't make any rash decisions when in desolation. On the contrary, Ignatius suggests, those times call for renewed emphasis on prayer, fasting, and almsgiving—traditional practices by which we unite our hearts with God. The way out of desolation is not by trying to escape from it but by aligning yourself to your guide and friend who will walk with you through it. The central symbol of Christian faith—the cross—is, among other things, a reminder that life involves suffering and even death. The good news, for followers of Jesus, is that suffering and death lose their "sting"—their power to plunge us forever into grief—because they become opportunities for God to exert comfort and power over death:

> Where, O death, is your victory?
> Where, O death, is your sting?
>
> —1 Corinthians 15:55

In a related vein, Viktor Frankl counsels that in the face of darkness, we ought to call to mind what gives meaning to our life: a person or an unfinished task that summons a renewed vigor to live in the face of hardship. Frankl recounts the story of one of his patients, a doctor who was experiencing severe depression after

the death of his beloved wife two years earlier. Frankl asked him
what might have happened if he had been the first to die, and the
man answered that his wife would have suffered terribly. Frankl
responded that he had spared his wife that suffering by outliv-
ing her; his responsibility now lay in surviving and mourning her.
Frankl reports that the man was fundamentally changed as a result
of this new insight.

> *Have you had an experience of having to navigate suffering?*
> *How did you do it?*
> *Are you in the midst of suffering? Who are the people who*
> *are there for you?*

Both Frankl and Ignatius remind us of a difficult yet beautiful truth:
no experience, however horrific, is the final word in a meaningful
life. Every person will experience suffering. To deny that fact—or
worse, to run away from it by turning to various pleasures—is to
avoid what might be an experience that gives birth to a new chapter in one's life. The process might be difficult, but the hope is that
in reorienting ourselves toward that which gives life meaning—and
in finding solace in a God who walks with us through suffering
toward new life—we become not only stronger people but also people capable of helping others to navigate the inevitable difficulties of
their lives. We become more deeply capable of kinship. That, more
than achievements, honors, or riches, brings forth happiness. But as
Frankl reminds us, happiness is not something that we pursue for
its own sake. It ensues from a life oriented toward mission, yielding
new forms of kinship with God and others.

NEXT STEPS:

If you're struggling to figure out what you're called to do, try a few of these simple steps:

1. Take out some paper and jot down or draw the experiences that made you feel most alive. What brought you the most joy? What times brought out your greatest strengths? Try to get everything down without judging what comes out. Afterward, take a look at these experiences. Do you see any patterns? Are any particular qualities mentioned more than others?

2. What is the "why" you're living for? Who or what brings you the most joy? If you had to name one thing you'd live for, what would it be?

3. St. Ignatius counsels us to ask for the grace we seek in prayer. The next time you pray, even if it's been a while, try asking God for exactly what you want. If you're trying to figure out your life's vocation, ask God for help. Ask God for the grace and clarity you need to shine light on your path.

4. If you're in a time of darkness, or desolation, feeling stuck and unable to figure out where to go next, heed St. Ignatius's other advice: act against. The saint calls us to act against any impulse that tries to drag us down or veer us from our path. Fight the impulse that takes you away from your course. Little by little, these small steps will help you out of your rut—even if it means just taking a walk, calling an old friend, cooking, or listening to music.

4

PRACTICE KINSHIP

For those who want to save their life will lose it, and those who lose their life for my sake will save it.
—Luke 9:24

For I greet him the days I meet him, and bless when I understand.
—Gerard Manley Hopkins, SJ, "The Wreck of the Deutschland"

Every vocation is rooted in love—not the vague love for a cause or an ideology but the very concrete love of people with real needs who have a deep urge to serve. *New York Times* columnist David Brooks uses the phrase "the summoned life" to suggest a similar idea about a vocation: others can bring out your gifts and talents, which you can in turn use to serve them. Both the word "summoned" and the word "vocation" (from the Latin *vocatus* "called") come from passive verbs, which, as grammarians know, always beg the question "summoned by whom?"

> *Who summons from you your greatest self?*

The easy answer might be that God brings out our gifts and talents, which in turn fuels our passion. But sometimes it's hard to know if we are responding to God's call or to our own passions. The two aren't always the same thing. People can be passionate about making money, advancing a political cause, or creating a work of art. But these pursuits might be rooted in selfish desires and prove destructive in the long run. Even in the early Church, we can see examples of people who were passionate about something, even believing that they were serving God, only to learn later that they were misguided. According to the Acts of the Apostles, Saul was a passionate follower of the law of Moses, but he was also murderous in his persecution of the followers of Jesus. Only after a profound conversion did Saul come to see Jesus differently, later becoming the apostle we now call St. Paul. Saul had passion, but it was misdirected.

Passion can be a good thing—and we need passion to live out our vocation—but it can also be rooted in a skewed understanding of reality. Members of hate groups are passionate; people on opposite sides of a political issue can be equally passionate. What is necessary for finding our true calling is conversion, in the sense of turning toward a greater truth with passion.

The most fundamental conversion we can experience, often as young people, is the one from selfishness to love. Growing up, we naturally tend to focus on our own needs. We desire popularity; we desire to be athletes or actors or great musicians; we desire to fit in and have all the things our peers have, from phones to clothes to cars. As we grow older, though, hopefully we learn something about love: about being generous to siblings, reaching out toward grandparents or other relatives, being there for our friends. And as we mature, many of us become more selfless by entering into relationships that teach us how to really care for another person. By the time some of us become parents or care for another person, hopefully we have learned a few lessons about sacrifice and meaning.

But beyond that fundamental conversion, there must follow many others. Some are intellectual, when we experience subtle shifts in our thinking that come from a greater grasp of reality. Education can broker such intellectual conversions, as we begin to gain more expansive understandings of the world and our place in it. Other conversions may be moral ones: we discern a new way of living in the world that makes us reconsider our choices, actions, and habits. Going on a diet, starting a new exercise regimen, reading a book or learning a language—all these are examples of moral conversions. We discern a good that summons from us new ways of acting. Still other conversions are more properly spiritual: they involve new understandings of who God is or who you understand yourself to be. Encounters with beauty, or suffering or death, or falling in love—these can be catalysts for spiritual conversions. Finally, there are religious conversions, which urge us to join communities with traditions, rituals, and practices that sustain our faith.

> *What experiences have awakened passion in you to serve others?*
> *When has a story in the news broken your heart or given you renewed hope?*
> *When have you become aware of another's vulnerability? When have you become aware of your own?*

Notice that there can be a great deal of flexibility in these different forms of conversion. I may have a new insight about God by reading St. Augustine or Julian of Norwich, but that intellectual conversion may have little impact on how I live my life or treat other people. Alternatively, I may develop a passion for service that has little influence on my willingness to go to church. An authentic life will certainly involve many conversions, but it is impossible to predict what having an openness to conversion will mean concretely in people's lives. Rather, such openness simply means that we do not close off the possibility of God speaking to us in new and perhaps surprising ways. What is fundamental is our willingness to practice living in ways that constantly open us to that possibility. In the words of the theologian John Henry Newman, "In a higher world it is otherwise, but here below to live is to change, and to be perfect is to have changed often."

CALLED TO LOVE

An authentic life—a life lived as you most truly are, as the person God has created you to be—is open to the possibility of falling in love in a profound way. It is a life ready for the discovery of oneself as a gift to others. Pedro Arrupe, a former superior of the Jesuits, articulates this hope beautifully:

> Nothing is more practical than finding God, that is, than falling in love in a quite absolute, final way. What you are in love with, what seizes your imagination, will affect everything. It will decide what will get you out of bed in the morning, what you will do with your evenings, how you will spend your weekends, what you read, who you know, what breaks your heart, and what amazes you with joy and gratitude. Fall in love, stay in love and it will decide everything.

Arrupe himself had a profound insight into this kind of falling in love with God. He was serving as a missionary in Hiroshima, Japan, on the day that the atomic bomb fell, and he later wrote and spoke often about that experience:

> As I opened the door which faced the city, we heard a formidable explosion similar to the blast of a hurricane. At the same time doors, windows and walls fell upon us in smithereens. . . .
> I shall never forget my first sight of what was the result of the atomic bomb: a group of young women, eighteen or twenty years old, clinging to one another as they dragged themselves along the road. One had a blister that almost covered her chest; she had burns across half of her face, and a cut in her scalp caused probably by a falling tile, while great quantities of blood coursed freely down her face. On and on they came, a steady procession

numbering some 150,000. This gives some idea of the scene of horror that was Hiroshima. . . .

At five in the morning, we finally arrived at our destination and began our first treatments on the Fathers. In spite of the urgency of our work, we had first stopped to celebrate our Masses. Assuredly, it was in such moments of tragedy that we felt God most near to us. It is at such moments one feels in need of supernatural assistance.

For Arrupe, that supernatural assistance meant being called and graced to serve the victims of a terrifying weapon in ways for which there was no precedent. Thousands of people died in the weeks following the explosion, and Arrupe writes poignantly of the grim work of taking care of their remains:

It is at such times that one feels most a priest, when one knows that in the city there are 50,000 bodies which, unless they are cremated, will cause a terrible plague. There were, besides, some 120,000 wounded to care for. In light of these facts, a priest cannot remain outside the city just to preserve his life. Of course, when one is told that in the city there is a gas that kills, one must be very determined to ignore that fact and go in. And we did. And we soon began to raise pyramids of bodies and pour fuel on them to set them afire.

Arrupe and his fellow Jesuits went into an area of toxic gas and radiation in order to minister to those who were suffering. They were called to love in a radical way.

CALLED TO SERVE

Another example of being called to love in a profound way—to practice kinship with strangers in a situation of extremity—is that of a young man who was later honored by the president of the United States for his sacrifice in the wake of the tragedies of September 11, 2001. Welles Remy Crowther, the "man in a red bandanna," as the

New York Times called him, was seen going up the stairs at the World Trade Center when hundreds were heading downstairs to escape the inferno that would later lead to the building's collapse. At the time, no one knew who he was, but his story later came to be known as a remarkable one of generosity and self-sacrifice, one that was broadcast nationwide in an ESPN video called *The Man in the Red Bandana.*

Crowther, a 1999 graduate of Boston College, was working at the World Trade Center's South Tower when the plane hit. With many already killed, Crowther, the son of a firefighter, took charge, instructing people to head to the exits and helping others unable to do so. As a youth, Crowther had spent many hours at the Empire Hook & Ladder Company in his hometown of Upper Nyack, New York, and he always carried a red bandana with him to prevent smoke inhalation. There, in the South Tower, he escorted people down many flights of stairs to safety before heading back up the stairs to help others. One person he helped was Ling Young, who could tell people later only that the man who helped her had a red bandana and was carrying another woman on his back.

Young made it out of the building, but Crowther did not. He had left a voice-mail message for his mother, Alison, after the planes had crashed, but she had a terrible feeling that he did not make it out. She searched in vain for information about her son for many weeks, but it was not until a newspaper article described Young's story—and her mention of the red bandana—that Alison knew what had happened to him. She sent a picture of Welles to Young, who recognized him immediately.

Alison later spoke at a memorial for Welles and other firefighters from the Rockland Fire Training Center who died on September 11. She said, "Welles must have felt hugely fulfilled that day. He was not

Welles Crowther, equities trader. . . . He was Welles Crowther, fire-fighter."

Alison's testimony points to something about her son— that regardless of his job, he had a vocation to serve others—but she also gives us a clue about the nature of vocation. In serving others, we come to the deepest, most authentic discovery of ourselves. Kinship with others is the key to self-understanding.

LESSONS FROM GREG BOYLE

The Jesuit priest Greg Boyle articulates the meaning of *kinship*—his word for being in right relationship with others—better than anyone else I know. For more than thirty years, Boyle has worked at Dolores Mission Church in Los Angeles with former gang members, who teach him every day what havoc a lack of kinship can cause in people's lives. Boyle is the founder of Homeboy Industries, which began as a way to offer young men and women paths out of gang life, and that now includes Homeboy Bakery, Homeboy Silkscreen & Embroidery, Homeboy/Homegirl Merchandise, Homegirl Café & Catering, Homeboy Farmers Market, and Homeboy Diner at Los Angeles City Hall. Boyle is the recipient of many honors and awards, and he was the subject of Celeste Fremon's 2008 book *G-Dog and the Homeboys*. His own 2010 book *Tattoos on the Heart* was a *New York Times* best seller and named one of the best books of that year by *Publisher's Weekly*.

In *Tattoos on the Heart*, Boyle writes compellingly about the moral imperative to practice kinship. In his preface he describes it like this:

> In Africa they say "a person becomes a person through other people." There can be no doubt that the homies have returned me to myself. I've learned, with their patient guidance, to worship Christ as He lives in them. It's easy to echo Gerard Manley

Hopkins here, "For I greet him the days I meet him, and bless when I understand."

For Boyle, there was nothing more profound than the call to practice love among former gang members immersed in a still-violent world (by 2010 he had buried 168 young people). To echo Arrupe's words, this love has affected everything for him: he has become one with those he serves.

In the book, Boyle narrates many stories of the trying vocation to which he found himself called. It began with a moral conversion of his own while working in Bolivia among the poor, whom he describes as having "a privileged delivery system for giving me access to the gospel." He discovered a deep desire to continue working with the poor, and so rather than accept a position at a university, he was assigned as the youngest pastor ever at a parish located amid gang activity. He writes, "If Los Angeles was the gang capital of the world, our little postage-stamp-size area on the map was the gang capital of LA."

It was a tough calling. In response to the shootings that regularly claimed young lives, Boyle and others at Dolores Mission set up an alternative middle school. Fights were common; many administrators and teachers came and went, some after just a day or two. But the school signaled a new attitude at the parish: two elder women counseled fellow parishioners that gang members should be welcomed, because it was what Jesus would do. The parish became a place of forging new kinship, and with that kinship came a new sense of mission. The struggles of gang life—and the desire to leave gang life—took on a sense of urgency among Boyle's parishioners. They started helping gang members find jobs and paths out of violent hopelessness. They offered day care and helped clean up the neighborhood. And when a donor came forward with a desire to help their efforts, Boyle steered him toward buying an old bakery across the street from the church, thus launching the Homeboy Bakery.

What is striking about Boyle's stories is the depth of relationships that he describes. Boyle decries the common attitude that "some lives matter less than other lives," and he tells stories about young men and women who desire to live with dignity but who must overcome tremendous obstacles. One such life is that of Spider, a former gang member who lived in the projects with his sister after their parents had abandoned them. Boyle spends some time driving him home from a job secured through Homeboy Industries, wondering how he's doing. Spider describes the joy he takes in seeing his two children eat:

> "But, well . . . I don't eat. I just watch them eat. My lady she gets crazy with me, but I don't care. I just watch 'em eat. They eat and eat. And I just look at 'em and thank God they're in my life. When they're done eating and I know they're full, THEN I eat.
>
> "And the truth . . . sometimes there's food left and sometimes there isn't. *Tú sabes*," he says to me, putting his hand on my shoulder as I drive, "it's a Father thing."

Spider expresses what Boyle, echoing the poet John Ruskin, calls "the duty to delight." Having been deprived of food and fatherhood in his own youth, Spider delights in being able to provide both to his young children.

Another story is that of Willy, whom Boyle describes as "a charmer, a quintessential homie con man who's apt to coax money out of your ATM if you let him." Willy hits him up for money, and Boyle drives to a local ATM to try to help him out. Boyle urges Willy to stay in the car for safety's sake; Willy obliges but asks for Boyle's keys to play the radio. Boyle suggests that he use the time to pray instead. To his great surprise, he returns to find Willy pensive, saying that God told him to shut up and listen. Boyle presses him for what he has experienced:

> "So, son, tell me something," I ask. "How do you see God?"
>
> "God?" he says, "That's my dog right there."
>
> "And God?" I ask, "How does God see you?"
>
> Willy doesn't answer at first. So I turn and watch as he rests his head on the recliner, staring at the ceiling of my car. A tear falls down his cheek. Heart full, eyes overflowing. "God . . . thinks . . . I'm . . . *firme*."
>
> To the homies, *firme* means, "could not be one bit better."
>
> Not only does God think we're *firme*, it is God's joy to have us marinate in that.

Boyle identifies what is at work in these conversion stories: the homies developed a new self-understanding because of relationships that helped them see themselves in a new way. In Willy's case, turning to God enabled him to see himself not as a criminal but as a beloved child. His former passion for being a con artist melted into a desire to be the person God sees him to be.

For Boyle, kinship is the key not only to the gospel that Jesus preached; it's the key to a full life:

> I was brought up and educated to give assent to certain propositions. God is love, for example. You concede "God loves us," and yet there is this lurking sense that perhaps you aren't fully part of the "us." The arms of God reach to embrace, and somehow you feel yourself just outside God's fingertips.
>
> Then you have no choice but to consider that "God loves me," yet you spend much of your life unable to shake off what feels like God only embracing you begrudgingly and reluctantly. I suppose, if you insist, God has to love me too. Then who can explain this next moment, when the utter fullness of God rushes in on you—when you completely know the One in whom "you move and live and have your being," as St. Paul writes. You see, then,

that it has been God's joy to love you all along. And this is completely new.

For Boyle, God is kinship—a word that also describes the Greek word *agape* from the New Testament, which means a self-giving love, the love that God shows to his creatures. In Boyle's experience, the vague idea that God is self-giving love is not enough, for this idea alone remains abstract. Only when "the utter fullness of God rushes in on you," he writes, in an experience of being wholly loved, does the concept God become a living person with whom one can fall in love. We are summoned—called—to embody that kind of love when we practice kinship.

Boyle sees a different problem with many of the homies, though. For them, the key problem is shame: the deep, abiding self-hatred that negates the feeling that one is worthy of God's love. Boyle tells the story of Carmen, "a heroin addict, a gang member, street person, [and] occasional prostitute." Carmen barges in as Boyle is preparing to celebrate a baptism. He is in a hurry, but she begs for his help. Reflecting on her life, she describes her state of helplessness: she has been addicted to drugs; she is "known all over . . . nationwide." And in a moment of reflection, she names the most fundamental problem: "I . . . am . . . a . . . disgrace." And in that moment, Boyle acknowledges that he had mistaken Carmen for an interruption. Boyle sees Carmen's kind of internalized shame as the very antithesis of kinship. He writes, "There is a palpable sense of disgrace strapped like an oxygen tank onto the back of every homie I know," later asking how to overcome such a toxic sense of self: "How does one hang in there with folks, patiently taking from the wreck of a lifetime of internalized shame, a sense that God finds them (us) wholly acceptable?"

His answer is, effectively, to become transparent messengers of God's mercy, to humble ourselves in ways that make God's own kinship evident to those who have internalized shame:

> There is a longing in us all to be God-enthralled. So enthralled that to those hunkered down in their disgrace, in the shadow of death, we become transparent messengers of God's own tender mercy. We want to be seized by that same tenderness; we want to bear the largeness of God.

What gets in the way too often are false senses of self—masks that we wear to prove to the world that we are valuable. For the homies, those masks are often written in ink: tattoos that proclaim to the world how they wish to be identified. One that Boyle remembers clearly is that of Ramiro, whose forehead read "F——k the world" and who, like thousands of other homies, sought out Homeboy Industries' laser tattoo-removal service so that he might not ultimately be limited by that mask.

For many others, though, the false sense of self is provided by membership in a gang, which offers some affirmation, however twisted, in a world that offers them less than nothing—it tells them that they are fundamentally bad. Boyle points to kinship as that which most radically roots his faith in God: "I am helpless to explain why anyone would accompany those on the margins were it not for some anchored belief that the Ground of all Being thought this was a good idea." For him, kinship represents a way of being in the world that paradoxically allows for the discovery of self by virtue of being with others. Kinship manifests what Jesus meant in saying, "For those who want to save their life will lose it, and those who lose their life for my sake will save it." (Luke 9:24) Rather than building up our egos by looking nervously at what others are doing, we can discern an authentic way of life by asking how we might give ourselves in love to those who call forth our talents.

Am I called to practice self-giving love?

*Who are the people who summon from me a desire for
    kinship?*

*How might I use my talents to help others know that they
    are wholly loved?*

KINSHIP WITH WHOM?

In this chapter, we've encountered three stories about people who gave up their lives in loving service to others. In the first two cases, we saw examples of people whose lives were shaped by two related factors: training and circumstance. Both Arrupe and Crowther led from where they discerned their desires were leading them: the former, from medical training into Jesuit priesthood, and the latter, from equities trading to firefighting. In both cases, dramatic circumstances summoned their gifts in service to others. They were able to respond to extremity by simply being whom God had made them to be.

In the third case, Boyle discerned a calling to be with the poor. He took on an experience of living among the poor in Bolivia—very much outside the normal pattern of mimetic desire—and discovered a profound desire to serve others in poverty. Sometimes, this kind of willingness to try a new experience offers one the opportunity to discern a new form of authentic desire, a new kind of self-understanding.

Such is the story of Katharine Drexel (1858–1955), a wealthy woman from Philadelphia who exemplifies conversion from one kind of freedom to another. Drexel, whose uncle founded Drexel University and whose father was an investment banker, was raised in a family that prioritized kinship with the poor. During her childhood, for example, she traveled all over the United States with her parents and learned firsthand of the plight of Native Americans and African Americans. Her family regularly opened their home to distribute food and clothing and to help with rent. Upon her parents' deaths, Katharine and her sisters received a large fortune, which they began to use for the St. Francis Mission on South Dakota's Rosebud Sioux reservation.

In 1887, at the age of twenty-nine, Katharine and her sisters met Pope Leo XIII in a private audience. Raising concern for Native Americans and African Americans, she urged the Pope to action. His response surprised her: "What about you? What are you going to do?" Her response—which unfolded over the next sixty years of her life—was to become a nun, found a new order, and establish a new university (Xavier University of Louisiana) as well as nearly sixty schools and missions.

> *What about you? What are you going to do?*

Pope Leo's question to Katharine is God's question to each of us. What the pope recognized in the formidable woman before him was an expression of authentic desire to serve those who were left behind in a burgeoning industrial society. It is worth noting that Leo was the pope whose 1891 encyclical *Rerum Novarum* (known in English as "On the Condition of Labor") is often cited as launching the modern tradition of Catholic social teaching—that is, of inviting the Church to pay attention to situations in the modern world that call for compassion and justice. Pope Leo had a heart for reaching out to the masses of people whom the Industrial Revolution left behind: millions of exploited workers with little power to escape poverty. When he met Katharine, he met someone who had similarly developed a compassionate heart and who experienced a profound desire to use her material and spiritual gifts to improve the lives of others.

One important clue to discovering our authentic desire is the direction of our compassion: Whom does our heart call us to love? Who calls us to the vocation to kinship? Especially in this digital age, we can know any number of people who cry to heaven for compassion. We don't need to be from a family like the Drexels, who could afford to bring their children on monthlong trips to faraway places. We can know about problems across town or across the world in an instant. Yet in having such immediate access to information, our hearts can become numb to the scale of the world's problems. So how, then, can we discern where God is leading us to express kinship in transformative ways?

There is certainly no one-size-fits-all answer to this question. There are examples of people who, like Arrupe or Crowther, respond to an immediate need. But even their stories are ultimately about discerning a vocation over a lifetime that enables them to be ready for that need. There are also examples of people like Boyle and Drexel whose formative experiences contributed to a lifelong discernment of how to serve those with whom they have entered into kinship.

Most of us will live rather ordinary lives characterized by family, friendship, work, volunteering, or some combination of any of these. A good life is not the same as a "great life," if by that we mean something that will be recorded in a history book or inscribed on a plaque. There is a famous—albeit dismal—comment by Henry David Thoreau from his meditative book *Walden*: "The mass of men lead lives of quiet desperation." I suggest a more hopeful approach: The mass of people lead lives of quiet sanctity. They understand the need to make their lives meaningful, to practice friendship, to show love to family, to contribute to their community. This is not to say that they are without sins and limitations; it is rather to say that their hearts respond to the immediate situations of people around them—family members, neighbors, fellow citizens. It was Mother Teresa of Calcutta, echoing a sentiment of St. Thérèse of Lisieux, who observed that not all of us can do great things, but we can all do small things with great love. And that, I suggest, is the way to begin discerning one's call to kinship.

NEXT STEPS:

1. In discerning our call to kinship, it can be helpful to jot down or draw pictures of past experiences of solidarity and service. Think about the times you have served others. What memories bubble up? Choose one and describe or capture it on paper.

2. What drove you to these acts of service? Why did you feel called to serve?

3. What was the experience like? What feelings did it bring out of you? Who or what made you feel full or alive? Was it a particular cause or a group of people? Try to identify what made you feel passionate.

4. Make a list of five different places or people you can serve now. Are there any organizations nearby that you can serve with your unique gifts and talents? Or is there a specific person in need? Try to pick one of your five, and then jot down how you will bring that desire to life.

5

LOVE FREELY

The main thing is not to hold on to anything.
—Dorothy Day

If the starting point for discernment is the desire to reach out in kinship toward others, its fruition is a life in which we are free to give fully of ourselves to others. In a word, a discerned life always moves us toward mercy. In Shakespeare's beautiful words:

'The quality of mercy is not strained;
It droppeth as the gentle rain from heaven
Upon the place beneath. It is twice blest;
It blesseth him that gives and him that takes.

Mercy is our heart's desire, whether we are the one who gives or the one who takes. Yet many things can get in the way of mercy: stress, busyness, and prejudice, to name a few. This chapter asks us how we can deepen our commitment to the practices of discernment so that we might remove these obstacles and experience "the quality of mercy" that comes from loving freely.

Our first clue on how to love freely comes from Dorothy Day, the founder of the Catholic Worker movement. In her younger years in the 1920s, Day was a bohemian political activist and writer, stirred by Marxism and the desire to topple the economic divide between rich and poor. But in her moving autobiography *The Long Loneliness*, she describes the natural happiness she derived upon becoming a mother and the process that ultimately led her to a spiritual conversion and entrance into the Church. Day started the first Catholic Worker house in order to practice a radical commitment to loving the poor as Jesus did, and she spent the rest of her life leading the movement that today includes nearly 250 communities in the United States and in twelve countries around the world. Dorothy Day teaches us something profound about loving freely—that is, about not letting anything get in the way of our kinship with others.

In 1954, Day wrote an essay called "Poverty and Precarity," reflecting on why members of her community took no salary:

> No one working with The Catholic Worker gets a salary, so our readers feel called upon to give and help us keep the work going. And then we experience a poverty of another kind, a poverty of reputation. It is said often and with some scorn, "Why don't they get jobs and help the poor that way? Why are they living off others, begging?"
>
> I can only explain to such critics that it would complicate things to give a salary to Roger for his work of 14 hours a day in the kitchen, clothes room, and office; to pay Jane a salary for running the women's house and Beth and Annabelle for giving out clothes, for making stencils all day and helping with the sick and the poor, and then have them all turn the money right back in to support the work. Or to make it more complicated, they might all go out and get jobs, and bring the money home to pay their board and room and the salaries of others to run the house. It is simpler just to be poor. It is simpler to beg. The main thing is not to hold on to anything.

For Day, the main thing that God asks of us is not to hold on to anything, because anything we withhold from God gets in the way of what God is trying to do in the world.

Jesus makes the same point in his counsel to the rich young man:

A certain ruler asked him, "Good Teacher, what must I do to inherit eternal life?" Jesus said to him, "Why do you call me good? No one is good but God alone. You know the commandments: 'You shall not commit adultery; You shall not murder; You shall not steal; You shall not bear false witness; Honor your father and mother.'" He replied, "I have kept all these since my youth." When Jesus heard this, he said to him, "There is still one thing lacking. Sell all that you own and distribute the money to the poor, and you will have treasure in heaven; then come, follow me." But when he heard this, he became sad; for he was very rich. Jesus looked at him and said, "How hard it is for those who have wealth to enter the kingdom of God!"

—Luke 18:18–24

Luke the Evangelist is particularly interested in the way that Jesus upends common conceptions of wealth and power. It is in Luke's Gospel that Jesus begins his ministry to "proclaim release to the captives and recovery of sight to the blind, to let the oppressed go free, to proclaim the year of the Lord's favor." (4:18–19) Luke refers to the poor almost as many times as the other three Gospels combined, seeing Jesus' entire ministry as characterized by liberating the poor from poverty and the rich from their slavery to possessions. Luke, whom Paul describes as a physician, accompanied the apostle Paul on his missionary journeys and so was certainly familiar with Paul's manner of speaking of Christ as the one who became poor so that people might become rich in the mercy of God: "For you know the generous act of our Lord Jesus Christ, that though he was rich, yet for your sakes he became poor, so that by his poverty you might become rich." (2 Corinthians 8:9)

What do I hold on to that may make it hard for me to enter the kingdom of God?

Does a desire for security or wealth crowd out my time for others?

Do I regularly interact with people who do not have the means that I have?

Do I make time to offer myself in service to those who need me?

It seems that people of Dorothy Day's time understood this dimension of Jesus' message about as much as people of Jesus' time did. It's not about the money—it's about the freedom to follow God completely. Money becomes a hang-up for many, though, because it exerts such a strong pull on our desires. Paul writes in his first epistle to Timothy, "The love of money is a root of all kinds of evil, and in their eagerness to be rich some have wandered away from the faith and pierced themselves with many pains." (6:10) Freedom from the desire for money amounts to a freedom to follow God wherever God leads us.

Now for a moment of transparency: I wrestle with this notion of freedom. I get the idea that money can become an end in itself; I get what Jesus is saying when he tells the apostles that we can't serve both God and money. But I'm a husband and a father, in the midst of caring for both children and an aging parent. So when I hear Jesus telling the disciple who wanted to say goodbye to his family before following him, "No one who puts a hand to the plow and looks back is fit for the kingdom of God" (Luke 9:62), I am challenged. Is Jesus saying that freedom is only for the single and unattached?

The reason I think that the answer is "no" is that I am too well convinced of the difficult, exquisite joy that the very young and the very old bring to our lives and of the need to work toward a culture that prizes, consoles, nurtures, and welcomes them. I read Jesus' words about total surrender to God's will against the larger backdrop of what he means by "the Kingdom," where all are called to be more like children (see Matthew 18:3, Luke 18:3, and Mark 10:13–16) and to honor our elders (as in Exodus 20:12, Proverbs 6:20, Sirach 3:6, Matthew 15:4, and Ephesians 6:2). And if we take God as a model for how to live in a community, we see someone who pays particular attention to children, someone who is lavish and even irresponsibly generous toward children. God is the Father who waits expectantly for the prodigal son to return, eager to throw a party in celebration (Luke 15:11–32). God is the Mother who holds her children close (in Matthew 23:37 and Luke 13:34). God makes us his children, waiting expectantly to pass along his kingdom to us as heirs (Romans 8:14–21).

Our attitude toward money, as toward all things, must aspire to the kingdom. Like the person who sells all to buy a field in which there is a buried treasure, so must we orient all our desires toward the kingdom and not withhold anything. For in the words of the psalmist, "Where can I go from your spirit? Or where can I flee from your presence?" (139:7) What part of our lives is somehow apart from God?

> *What is God's desire for the way I use my talents, money,*
> *   and time?*
> *What might God be asking me to let go of in order to be*
> *   freer to love?*
> *When do I see God in my relationships with others?*
> *If I were free from the desire for money, what good would I*
> *   want to do in the world?*

Our desire for money is good to the extent that it allows us to work toward the kingdom. In seeking to provide homes for the very young and very old, to provide food and education and other necessities of life, to build families and establish community relations—all these things are good. But there is yet a further invitation, rooted in a deeper desire.

THE DESIRE FOR GOD

Every good desire can become dangerous when we turn it excessively inward toward ourselves. The desire for nourishment can become gluttony; the desire for relationship can become lust; the desire for respect can become sinful pride. One of the traditional names for the devil is Lucifer—in Latin, "light bearer"—because of the recognition that unhealthy or disordered desires begin as desires for something that appears good but in reality has a dark side. What makes our desires disordered is a kind of myopia—a narrowing of vision such that we see only our immediate, selfish good rather than the larger reality in which we are a small part.

Many spiritual traditions have emphasized ascetic practices as ways to curb the pull toward disordered desires. The person who fasts, gives up a certain pleasure (smoking, drinking, social media), or takes on an extra task (babysitting, taking out the elderly neighbor's trash) refuses the temptation to satisfy immediate desires in order to act toward a more expansive vision of good.

And in seeking to satisfy every desire, there is an "opportunity cost." There are only so many hours in a day and only so many things a person can accomplish in life. We have to choose certain opportunities and give up others. And given the presence of so many desires at any given moment—bodily, psychic, spiritual, creative, and so on—how does a person discern which desires to act upon? The task of discernment is a creative one. For example, I might balance my daily desire for nourishment with my broader desire for relationship by asking a friend out to lunch. I might balance my desire for some quiet with my desire for learning by finding a place to read a good book. But at the same time, if I am always prioritizing immediate desires, I may not allow myself the time or energy to address more lasting concerns and deeper desires.

"Strive first for the kingdom," Jesus exhorts. (Matthew 6:33) I read this as Jesus saying that our first desire—both in terms of priorities in our lives and in terms of how we make decisions—must be to work with God to build a better world. Our first desire must not, then, be centered on ourselves but on God. How does this work?

Throughout this book, I've used the word "God" in rather traditional ways, pointing to the biblical use of the term to refer to the ancient Israelites' object of worship and to the person named by Jesus as Father. Of course, the same word "God" is used in other religious traditions, as well as in philosophical treatments of big questions such as where the cosmos originated. In speaking of a desire for God, though, I want to be more precise in what I mean. We are asking the same question that St. Augustine asked in his autobiography: What do I desire when I desire God?

The eleventh-century theologian St. Anselm of Canterbury offers us an answer. In his work *Proslogion* ("Discourse"), he describes himself as someone "who strives to lift his mind to the contemplation of God, and seeks to understand what he believes." In other words, he begins with a kind of wonder rooted in desire, and he reflects upon that experience in order to find some measure of understanding. To desire God is to "lift the mind," if we follow Anselm's idea. There is a long genealogy of this idea, from Anselm to St. Augustine and back to the philosopher Plato. For them, God is to be described in superlatives: "highest," "best," "most excellent," "most perfect," and so on. God is the sum of all perfections. He is, in the words of the poet Rainer Maria Rilke, "the ever-greater One."

What I desire when I desire God is that which will satisfy my deepest longings for goodness, for truth, and for beauty. Any time I am stirred to seek justice—whether it be racial justice, justice for prisoners, justice for immigrants, or justice for wage earners—I am seeking relationships that bear God's image. Any time I seek truth—whether it be the truth of the human person, the truth of history's vagaries, the truth about who I really am, or the truth about what Jesus' mission was—I am seeking to know certainties about the world that exists because God has loved it into existence. Any time I am stirred by beauty—whether the beauty of heroic sacrifice, the beauty of a sublime work of art, or the beauty of the natural world around me—I behold shadows of the deepest reality of God. My deepest longings reach toward God. The inner compass of my desires finds its true north in God. God is, in the words of the theologian Michael Buckley, "the direction toward which wonder progresses," the magnet that exerts a pull on the iron filings of my imagination. All true desires lead us to God.

> *When have I experienced desires for greater justice, greater mercy, greater beauty than what I ordinarily see in the world?*
> *When has my heart been broken?*

In contrast, sin orients us toward a smaller version of ourselves. Sin is disrupted desire. It is desire that sets out on a long journey and then gives up after a mile. It is desire that longs for beauty but settles for what's popular. It is desire that steels us for excellence but rests easy in satisfaction.

Sin is a "failure to bother to love," in the words of the theologian James Keenan. Keenan draws from an essay by the theologians David Burrell and Stanley Hauerwas that tells the story of Albert Speer, an architect whom Hitler hired to bring efficiency to the machinations of war. Speer was eager to please his superiors and provide for his family, and he was eventually promoted to a position in which he developed more efficient ways to bring weapons to the front lines of a collapsing Nazi army. Keenan points to Speer as an extreme example of the ways that our moral horizons can become small as a result of stunted desire. Speer was like many of us, desiring a good life for himself and his family and hoping for affirmation from those around him. He failed, though, to bother asking the bigger questions: What is the meaning of my work? What good is my labor contributing to? Is it possible that my work may be harming the world? His failure to raise such questions and instead focusing on what was immediately good for himself was rooted in disordered desire.

DOWNWARD MOBILITY

The Jesuit priest Dean Brackley proposes an antidote to the peculiarly Western form of disordered desire. After serving as a professor for a number of years in New York, Brackley made the difficult choice to spend the rest of his professional career at the Universidad Centroamericana in El Salvador. His Jesuit predecessors there had been brutally murdered in 1989 by a corrupt political regime that believed the Jesuits' work stirred up the poor of that country. In replacing them, Brackley chose a life of kinship with a poor population whose hope was the education that the Jesuits provided at the university. He calls this antidote "downward mobility," describing it this way:

> For we live out our relationship to God in relationship to the world—principally in relation to others and secondarily in relationship to things. It is true that attachment to God depends on a kind of detachment from riches and honors, but it depends more on attachment to people, especially the poor and outcast. The way of the world is upward mobility, a flight from the poor. The way of Christ is downward mobility, a quest for ever more

authentic solidarity with the poor. Avarice and honors are the first dangers to this solidarity because they lead us away from the poor; poverty and humiliations, on the other hand, cement the friendship.

Brackley highlights a kind of sickness that can threaten the full flowering of our authentic selves: namely, a desire for possessions as well as for the esteem of others that can cause us to focus on ourselves rather than on God. The cure, Brackley suggests, is kinship with the poor and outcast. Such kinship helps us to arrange our priorities, pulling us out of ourselves to see the world more clearly. People—and especially needy people—are the face of God, and to the extent that we create obstacles that get in the way of our seeing them as we see ourselves, we limit our freedom in favor of an idol, a false god.

This idol is rooted in the good desire to have a meaningful life. It becomes disordered when the desire for meaning turns selfish rather than opening us toward the vastness of friendship with others, especially those who have nothing to offer but themselves. The grace of seeing another person not as a means to some end that serves me—*my* social capital, *my* sexual satisfaction, *my* political connection—but rather as a *person* is the grace of encountering the ever-greater One.

Too often, we—all of us, myself included—see other people through the lens of cultural symbols. He wears these kinds of clothes; she has this profession; he went to that university; she has that prestigious job. We determine what a person means to us on the basis of these social cues. "What do you do for a living?" "Where did you go to school?" "Where are you from?" These often innocuous questions probe how we, in our insecurity, measure ourselves against our interlocutors. We talk about where we've traveled, or what social media-worthy experiences we've had, or what things we think might make us appear valuable to others. But each of those deposits in the banks of our social capital may in fact make us less and less able to enter into friendship with those who lack such capital. Perhaps these acts of insecurity that drive us to the top of the social ladder make us less free and less able to be our true selves and instead draw us deeper into the isolation of a false self. The answer is to take a long, loving look at persons who show us the face of God.

PERSONS

The word "person" comes from the Latin *persona*, meaning "to sound through." In the ancient world, an actor would wear a mask through which he would "sound" the character, whom the audience came to know by his words and actions. Today while watching a play, we attend to the person on the stage, await the revelation of her story, and are drawn into every emotion, from sadness to joy to anger to fear, by watching the character closely. In a good play, the person reveals not only herself but also something about ourselves.

In Jewish and Christian traditions, humans reflect God's image, and the world is their stage to "sound through" their person. Of course, no human being can come to know everyone on that stage, but all of us have the opportunity to know some of them. Which ones? Whom do we seek out? Who are the people who will broker an encounter with the ever-greater One? Certainly, as children we come to know the members of our families most intimately. As we grow, though, we develop more and more freedom to decide whom we will spend time with. If we follow the examples of Jesus and the saints, we ought to be seeking out those on the margins, for they point us toward God. They have, as we saw from Greg Boyle in chapter 4, "some privileged delivery system for giving [us] access to the gospel." In learning to see them as persons just like us, we come to know our authentic selves.

The great moral challenge of our age is to develop practices and habits that constitute a spirituality of encounter with people, to really see them. The Zulu greeting *sawubona*, "I see you," suggests something of this spirituality. It signifies a willingness to contemplate the personhood of another. To see another—eye to eye, as it were—is to act with reverence rather than utility. Too often the way we "see" others is as objects to be manipulated: cashiers who are supposed to process things quickly; drivers who are in our way; workers who make our lives hard; sexual partners meant to satisfy our small bodily desires; refugees who might compromise our lifestyles; members of another race portrayed poorly in movies; political opponents; tax collectors, lepers, prostitutes, and sinners. To really say to another person "I see you" is to first recognize that God has made that person and loves him or her no less than God loves you, and that before all else is worthy of your reverence, respect, awe, and wonder.

It is interesting to note that the related word *sakubona*, which means "we see you," is used in the Xhosa translation of the Gospel of Matthew. This greeting, in a way, helps us grasp what it means to really "see" the person as a person:

> Then the righteous will answer him, "Lord, when was it that we *saw you* hungry and gave you food, or thirsty and gave you something to drink? When was it that we *saw you* a stranger and welcomed you, or naked and gave you clothing? And when was it that we *saw you* sick or in prison and visited you?"
> —Matthew 25:37–39 (emphasis added)

Jesus' answer, of course, is that whenever we see a person in need and address him or her, we see Christ. The Xhosa translation of Matthew 25, a cornerstone of Christian social ethics, suggests that what it means to really see another person as a person is to have a willingness to be vulnerable before their vulnerability, to embrace their suffering as your own, knowing that as human beings we share a fragile state. "How small that is, with which we wrestle, / What wrestles with us, how immense," writes Rilke. When we say "I see you," we enter into kinship with another person. We no longer see that person as an object. We see the face of God.

Both Zulu and Xhosa are Bantu languages of southern Africa, and as such they manifest the Bantu humanist philosophy of *ubuntu*. Loosely translated as "human kindness," *ubuntu* reflects a conviction that "a person is a person through other people." Desmond Tutu describes it this way:

> Ubuntu [is] the essence of being human. Ubuntu speaks particularly about the fact that you can't exist as a human being in isolation. It speaks about our interconnectedness. You can't be human all by yourself, and when you have this quality—Ubuntu—you are known for your generosity. We think of ourselves far too frequently as just individuals, separated from one another, whereas you are connected and what you do affects the whole World. When you do well, it spreads out; it is for the whole of humanity.

Ubuntu can help us unmask a dominant social construct in our philosophically impoverished West: namely, the false belief that we are isolated actors in competition with one another over scarce resources. Only when we let go of our competitiveness can we begin to see persons not as obstacles but as companions on a pilgrimage.

INTEGRATED PERSONS

Coming to see others as partners rather than competitors, though, can mean living against the grain. A colleague once observed that on college campuses, "We have become parts of people relating to parts of people." The same can be said about society at large. In an age of technology and specialization, our societies have become fragmented. We have become adept at switching out personas—masks—in various circumstances: here I am a son, here an employee, here a husband, here a political position, here a religious affiliation, and so on. This fragmentation has come at a very high social cost: we have a diminished sense of the integrated self, as well as a diminished sense of connection with other integrated persons. I may care about the people at work, for example, but to really care for them as whole persons can strike many as transgressing social norms or protocols.

> *Do I really know the people I see on a daily basis?*
> *Do I seek to understand my classmates, coworkers, teachers,*
> *partners, or superiors?*
> *Do I know the challenges they face, the people they love, the*
> *causes they care about?*
> *Do I seek to really see the people I interact with? To see them*
> *as God sees them?*
> *Do I allow others to really see my true self?*

Jean Vanier, the founder of L'Arche, the international federation of communities for the intellectually disabled, was the winner of the 2015 Templeton Prize, a prestigious award that honors an individual who has made an exceptional contribution to spirituality. In his many writings as a theologian and philosopher, Vanier describes the challenge we face in overcoming fragmentation and engaging others as whole persons:

> Power and cleverness call forth admiration but also a certain separation, a sense of distance; we are reminded of who we are not, of what we cannot do. On the other hand, sharing weaknesses and needs calls us together into "oneness." We welcome into our heart those who love us. In this communion, we discover the deepest part of our being: the need to be loved and to have someone who trusts and appreciates us and who cares least of all about our

capacity to work or to be clever and interesting. When we discover we are loved in this way, the masks or barriers behind which we hide are dropped; new life flows. We no longer have to prove our worth; we are free to be ourselves. We find a new wholeness, a new inner unity.

Vanier challenges us to see what is most essential to our personhood. It is not the validation of others, which may come in any number of ways, from money to admiration to fame to professional advancement. All of these arise out of societal pressures for objects that are deeply unsatisfying. Rather, Vanier reminds us of the need to be loved and the freedom we find when we allow ourselves to grow into the wholeness that love nurtures.

One of the many people whom Vanier's movement touched was Henri Nouwen (1932–1996), a priest-psychologist who was a tenured professor at Yale. After a difficult stint teaching at Harvard, he sought a different path; he was successful in his teaching and writing but found himself emotionally exhausted: "It was one of the hardest places I'd ever been. It's an ambitious school, sometimes even somewhat arrogant. I didn't know how to deepen my heart and my soul, how to stay close to Jesus in the midst of it all." In an interview, he described to the author Arthur Boers what was happening in him and why he sought out Daybreak, the L'Arche community near Toronto:

> If [the handicapped people] express love for you, then it comes from God. It's not because you accomplished anything. These broken, wounded, and completely unpretentious people forced me to let go of my relevant self—the self that can do things, show things, prove things, build things—and forced me to reclaim that unadorned self in which I'm completely vulnerable, open to receive and give love regardless of any accomplishments.

What Nouwen discovered—like Vanier before him—is authentic love. Such a love is never "for" something else; it is freely given, unearned, undeserved, a gift, an overflow, a grace. Indeed, in Christian tradition, the very word "grace" means "gift," to suggest that wherever one encounters such love, one encounters the face of God. Authentic love can unfold only between people who are truly free.

The irony is that our mad rush for success, for reputation, for social standing, for prestige and honors, may be exactly the opposite of what we need. For if love is free, then everything we do to try to earn it gets in the way. Consider Jesus' paradoxical words:

> Blessed are you who are poor,
> for yours is the kingdom of God.
> Blessed are you who are hungry now,
> for you will be filled.
> Blessed are you who weep now,
> for you will laugh.
> Blessed are you when people hate you,
> and when they exclude you, revile you,
> and defame you
> on account of the Son of Man.
>
> —Luke 6:20–22

Jesus calls people to be merciful like the Father: to love others indiscriminately, even irresponsibly, without regard for any personal gain. He calls them to downward mobility, to embrace the graces of exclusion in order that they might develop selves free from social pressures and unhealthy desires. What many would call poverty Jesus calls freedom. For vessels that have been emptied of all pride are wide open and ready to receive love, and equally ready to pour it out in the love of others. They become persons who show the face of God. And they become capable of authentic friendship.

NEXT STEPS:

1. Can you think of a time when a work commitment or a relationship prevented you from being present to someone? Is there something that you held on to too tightly—a relationship, a job for its security, an unhealthy habit, a desire for advancement? How did that affect your relationship with others? Did it stop you from seeing the person as a fellow human being?

2. Do you have qualms about that situation? How do you feel about it now?

3. What do you want to tell God about your actions? What do you want to tell God about your desires? What do you want to ask God for?

4. Bring all of these thoughts to God in prayer. Ask for the grace you need to see fellow beings as persons, not competitors, and to detach from things you clench on to so that you can be open to God's call to love freely.

6

BE A FRIEND

The real love of man must depend on practice, and therefore, must begin by exercising itself on our friends around us, otherwise it will have no existence. By trying to love our relations and friends, by submitting to their wishes, though contrary to our own, by bearing with their infirmities, by overcoming their occasional waywardness by kindness, by dwelling on their excellences, and trying to copy them, thus it is that we form in our hearts that root of charity, which, though small at first, may, like the mustard seed, at last even overshadow the earth.

—John Henry Newman

If we discern a desire to love freely, there is no more perfect way to practice it than through friendship. Friendship, according to the twelfth-century monk Aelred of Rievaulx, who wrote a treatise on the subject, is a window to seeing God. For in friendship we practice the giving of ourselves and the receiving of another, discovering beauty along the way. Today, however, with our fast pace and tendency to overschedule, prioritizing building a relationship with a friend can seem time intensive and counterintuitive. Driven by social media, many of our friendships have become numerous but not very meaningful—leaving us hungering for depth.

An experience I had with one of my daughters made me think anew about this hunger for relationship and the often unsatisfying ways we try to fulfill it. A few years ago, I took my then-fifth-grade daughter to a talk given by a nutritionist. The fifth graders had recently begun a running and fitness program designed to encourage habits of exercise and wellness, and this talk was organized to help the girls think about their eating habits.

The nutritionist's basic point was that the girls should strive to take in three of the four food groups at every meal and not stress too much over the occasional desire for something sweet. But she mentioned a point that has stuck with me ever since: The craving for sweets happens when our bodies don't get the nutrients they really need. Lacking the right nutrients, they crave the most basic, simple sugars for instant calories and energy.

My takeaway: when we don't get what we need, we start craving.

I tested that thesis on myself and my children in the ensuing weeks. I made a point of encouraging healthy eating and snacking and watched both my own moods and those of my children, and I noticed something.

First, I became painfully aware of the fact that I turn into a diva when I'm hungry. I get irritable and short tempered, no matter how hard I try, usually snapping at someone I love. It was a humbling discovery.

Second, I started to notice that my children were generally happier and not as prone to tantrums or anger at each other or at me and my wife. I found that our quality of life improved when their blood sugar wasn't out of whack.

Third, I started to pay attention to the fact that in our busy lives, it's not always possible to keep our respective tanks full of nutrients. Some weeks were too busy for thorough food shopping; some days were too crowded for preparing decent meals; sometimes we just forgot until late in the day, when (in the midst of a tantrum) we realized that our diet that day had been atrocious.

I began to connect the dots: Our bodies lack what they need, and so we start craving the most easily accessible sugars. We become irritable and easily angered, and our relationships with one another suffer. We lash out even as we withdraw into our own shells, or plug ourselves into some sort of screen (TV, computer, phone). Lost in our own worlds, we fail to do the normal things to keep life moving smoothly—laundry, cleaning up, homework, and so on—and so we fall behind. We feel rushed, fail to plan our meals well, and the cycle repeats. Ugh.

When we don't get what we need, we start craving.

What is true of our bodies is equally true of our souls. Human beings are stitched together with the stuff of heaven, and this stuff cries out in our waking hours to be connected to one another.

I see a similar contrast between the nourished body and the craving body, the nourished soul and the craving soul. The nourished soul rests in the comfort of loving and being loved, of knowing intuitively that it dwells in the presence of God because it experiences this love firsthand. The craving soul, however, seeks out versions of love, the simple sugars of compliments, or Facebook likes, or text messages from acquaintances, or meaningless sex. Love nourishes us, but superficial affirmations give us only temporary highs. Our souls suffer from the same problems that beset our bodies: we are pressed for time, we get into unhealthy patterns of behavior, we slowly suffocate ourselves, and we reach out for what is easiest to get hold of.

Americans are obese at rates unheard of in earlier generations; many cannot understand or control their bodies' cravings. Similarly, Americans are disconnected from one another in thoroughly modern ways; we cannot understand or control our souls' cravings. So as a culture, we see evidence of our inability to form friendships that nourish us:

- More people are living alone than ever before, according to US census data.
- We have lots of sex, but many of us are unable to stay married to the same person. The divorce rate remains at about half of all marriages, but fewer and fewer people even attempt to marry someone today.
- We are lonelier than ever. The psychiatrists Jacqueline Olds and Richard S. Schwartz describe it this way: "Over the past decade, America has become an even lonelier country for many who live here. As psychiatrists, we recognize the toll this takes on people's health and well-being. . . . Americans fall into a trap of social isolation that is damaging emotionally, physically, and politically."

What is it, then, that we need most? What will nourish us? What will nourish our souls? What will help us to see our cravings as weak substitutes for love and relationships?

> *Who are your dearest friends?*
> *What is it about your friends that gives you joy? What do*
>   *you do to cultivate your friendships?*
> *Do you practice friendship on a daily basis?*
> *Do you feel like you have full and lasting friendships?*

COMPETITION

We think of friendship as one of the constants in human experience. Why, then, can it be hard to find a true, lifelong friend? Could it be that there are ways of thinking that hamper our ability to reach out to be friends with others?

Some years ago a student of mine—let's call her Abby—related a story that haunts me to this day, a story that illustrates to the extreme how messed up our ideas about friendship can be. Abby had traveled to Europe with two girlfriends, and the three of them were having the time of their lives seeing sights and meeting guys. One evening, though, Abby found herself alone with a guy who took advantage of her, leaving her feeling isolated and hurt. Sharing this experience with her friends the next day, she was wounded a second time: instead of reaching out with words of support, her friends accused Abby of ruining their good time. For the rest of the trip, she could feel a rift growing between her and the other two. By the time they got home, Abby could barely tolerate seeing them. Later, when the three returned to school, Abby learned that these two "friends" had spread the word that she had ruined their entire trip by sharing a sob story.

Abby related this story to me during a course in which we were investigating ancient and modern understandings of friendship. We had just read Aristotle's treatment of friendship, and Abby came to realize that her former friends were merely what he called "friends of pleasure." Abby named the problem: she had taken away their fun by reporting to them that something bad had happened. Things were suddenly no longer fun, and she was the cause.

Not long into telling me this story, Abby was weeping. Her realization was coupled with a difficult self-assessment: "If my friends are just people that I'm having fun with, what happens if the fun goes away?" Abby understood that there has to be something more substantial to a relationship if it's going to really mean something and last through the ordinary ups and downs of life.

What is a true friend? How can you find one? How can you be one? These are questions that lie dormant in the soul—dormant in the sense that they are what our souls hunger for but are often unable to name—very much like our hunger for God. Just as a vitamin deficiency might show up as fatigue or susceptibility to catching a cold, so too a friendship deficiency might show up as an unwillingness to trust other people, or a difficulty identifying people whom you want to share life's ups and downs with honestly. Our bodies don't tell us, "You're missing vitamin C!" any more than our souls scream out, "Learn how to love!" And yet in both cases, supplying the missing piece results in greater flourishing. On the other hand, supplying the wrong piece—like sugar for our bodies or hookup sex for our souls—just makes the problem worse.

The problem is that when we're surrounded by cultural messages that are all about the sugar or the shallow relationship, it's hard to see through the mental fog. It's hard to name what our souls really yearn for, except perhaps in those moments when we become conscious of our loneliness. And too often, we dismiss these bad feelings by doing something that distracts us, and we don't really ask ourselves what our lives are missing.

What makes true friendship difficult to find is the fact that we train ourselves for competition, not cooperation. From the playground to the schoolroom to the athletic field to the corporate office, we are bred to be winners. In such a context, it's easy to consider anyone who is on my side, anyone who shares my goal, anyone who is willing to help me succeed, as a friend. What Abby realized was that her former friends weren't really into knowing her (or each other, probably). They just had their eyes on a good time. As long as Abby helped them have fun, all was fine. But the moment she got in the way of their good time, she was a competitor, a hurdle to get over.

The difference between a false friend and a real friend is that there is no competition with a real friend. There is only delight in each other's company and a recognition that life with all its ups and downs is better with the friend than without.

Let me suggest another story to illustrate this idea. It comes from a friend's eleven-year-old son—we'll call him Ted—who not long ago transferred to a new middle school. Ted had friends at his old school and missed them after the transfer. He didn't know anyone yet at the new school and was lonely. Wanting to reconnect with his old friends, Ted went back to the old school to visit, only to discover that the dynamics had changed. He felt outside the circle of what had once felt familiar, and he discovered that his old friends weren't as willing to schedule time with him. It was as if he had once been part of a circle, but once removed, the circle had closed. Ted had thought that these were his good friends, but now he no longer felt all that important. His "value" as a friend had dropped as a result of changing schools. When he was in the circle, he had social value—he helped his friends feel good about being there; they enjoyed one another's company; maybe they helped each other with schoolwork. But once he was out of the circle, he competed for his former friends' time and attention, which they judged would be better spent on others still at the school. And this realization was very difficult for him.

Is Ted's situation all that different for us grown-ups in our various jobs and social arrangements? Don't we, too, fall prey to thinking of others (or being thought of by others) in terms of their social value? As in, "Is it worth my time and energy to build this relationship?"

There are many reasons why our friendships fall into patterns of competition and why some people seem to overcome these patterns and develop good friendships. I could talk about economic instability, geographic mobility, entertainment worship, incivility in the public square, breakdown in families, or the demand for upward mobility. But what I want to talk about instead is something we have lost: the sense that authentic friendship means sharing a pilgrimage toward what is good, true, and beautiful—a notion the ancients understood and one that we would do well to recover.

FRIENDSHIP AND VIRTUE

The ancient Greek philosopher Aristotle observed that friendship was of such central importance to human life that without it, one could scarcely choose to live at all. He named three fundamental types of friendship—or, to be more precise, two incomplete models of friendship and one complete model. The first incomplete model is *friendship of utility*, as with coworkers whom we may be happy to see on a regular basis but who are relatively easy to forget when we no longer work together. The second incomplete model is *friendship of pleasure*: we enjoy being with certain people but do not have a strong desire to be in a close relationship with them. The only real friends, Aristotle suggested, are *friends of virtue*: people who walk with us through life toward what is truly good, making life rich and meaningful along the way. It is with these friends that we come to learn what is most worth desiring in life.

The ancient Greeks told a paradigmatic story of two friends, Damon and Pythias, who dedicated themselves to the teachings of the philosopher Pythagoras. Their teacher called his followers to live lives of discipline and generosity, calming their selfish desires by practicing sharing all things in common and pursuing truth as disciples. Through years of this practice, Damon and Pythias had forged a bond of friendship, sustained by a shared belief that their chosen way of life enabled a common happiness that was greater than either could achieve alone. In solitude, each had pursued truth; but together, they had found happiness.

They lived, though, in the land of Syracuse, ruled by a cruel and jealous tyrant named Dionysius. When Dionysius suspected that Pythagoras's follower Pythias was plotting against him, he moved swiftly. Whether Pythias was truly guilty we can never know; it is more likely that he expressed some displeasure with the tyrant's rule. In any case, Dionysius immediately sentenced Pythias to death. Pythias begged him for the chance to put his affairs in order and bid farewell to his family, but Dionysius would not budge.

Damon, upon hearing of his friend's fate, went to Dionysius and said that he would take Pythias's place in prison until the time of the execution. Dionysius, astonished at the offer, let Pythias go, with the caution that should he fail to return, Damon would be executed in his place. Pythias pledged to return and set off with great speed.

The day of the execution drew near, and Pythias was nowhere to be found. Dionysius mocked Damon's naïveté, reminding him that he was to die in the absence of his friend. Yet Damon remained unmoved, even telling Dionysius that he hoped Pythias would not return but rather stay home with his family on a distant shore.

On the day of the execution, Dionysius was perplexed at Damon's equanimity. The two men proceeded toward the place where the execution would take place, when, minutes before the event, Pythias arrived on horseback, bedraggled and exhausted. He told the story of his trip home, followed by a return voyage in which he was thrown overboard by pirates. He had somehow managed to swim back to shore and find a horse to return to the palace.

Damon, now overcome with emotion upon seeing his friend, embraced him, and then turned to Dionysius: "Let him go and return home. You have me instead." Pythias, equally overcome, exhorted the king to deny his friend's request: "No, release my friend and take me."

Dionysius was stunned at this show of mutual generosity in the face of death. What had these Pythagoreans understood that so eluded him? How could they have come to such a place of mutual love that they ignored even the fear of death that constantly haunted the king?

"Enough," Dionysius said to the two men. "Neither of you shall be executed today. Instead you will stay on as my advisers and teach me what it is you have learned about friendship, and perhaps one day you will count me too as a true friend."

THE MYSTERY OF FRIENDSHIP

Friendship is at once a universal human experience and a mystery. Some of the most memorable ancient stories are about friendship—it has been the theme of poets, painters, and playwrights over the ages. People plan their lives and deaths around friendship and are quick to reflect on why their friends are more dear to them than money, work, power, or pleasure. If one of the friends in the story of Damon and Pythias were pressed to answer why he risked his life for the other, I suspect he would say, "Because he was my friend." We don't know what it is, but we know it when we experience it.

It is precisely the mysteriousness of friendship that makes it so desirable. It seems to be a good for its own sake that almost everyone would consider of great value. It touches our very humanness, and it raises questions about what that humanness is all about. To many, friendship is a doorway to talk about spirituality and about God, and the ways that our friendships imitate God: for true friendships are rooted in a shared faith of acting toward a good that may be unclear yet is worth pursuing together.

But even without such a perspective, we can acknowledge that friendship helps us discover parts of ourselves that we might not otherwise have known. It is perhaps for that reason that the ancient Greek biographer Diogenes Laërtius famously observed that a friend is like a single soul dwelling in two bodies. On some level, Pythias, the man who was to be executed, understood that the death of

Damon would be like the death of a part of himself, and vice versa. True friendship, he intuited, is unlike any of the other ways that humans express interests, likes, desires, yearnings, loves: friendship cuts deep into the heart and becomes grafted onto one's very identity. "Tell me what company you keep," wrote Cervantes, "and I'll tell you what you are."

If we follow the basic insight of Aristotle, friendship is the by-product of a shared pursuit of virtue. To put it a little differently, friendship isn't something you just happen upon, or the result of fate or chance or magic or chemistry or biology. It's something that emerges when people of like minds focus on another, greater pursuit. The original source of the Damon and Pythias story is the fourth-century Greek writer Aristoxenus, a student of Aristotle who wrote several texts about Pythagoras and his disciples and who might have been intrigued by the otherwise irrelevant detail that the friends were both Pythagoreans. Why is this important? Perhaps Aristoxenus saw in this detail proof of what Aristotle had suggested. The Pythagoreans were known for their almost monastic, quasi-spiritual practices, for their emphasis on mathematical harmony in the universe (including music, which Aristoxenus himself became known for much later). They were a community dedicated to seeking the truth of the cosmos.

To put it most simply, maybe Aristoxenus saw that the reason Damon and Pythias were capable of being friends is because they sought truth together, and each was able to grasp the truth more fully because of the other. And that kind of friendship was worth dying for.

FRIENDSHIP TODAY

While it is certainly true that many people reap the benefits of rich friendships, I often see a lingering feeling of loneliness among young people. In this age, when the word "friend" has become a nearly meaningless verb, signifying a virtual connection to everyone in general and no one in particular, it's worth asking how our understanding and practices of friendship have been shaped by modern, rapid cultural changes. We circle ourselves with dozens, even hundreds, of friends, both real and virtual. We check their status updates, we view their pictures, we marvel at their interesting life experiences. We categorize friends according to when we first knew them: here are friends from school or college; here are people from work. We develop a barometer of how close friends are—those who are mere acquaintances and those who are in our inner circle (with ourselves, of course, at the center of it).

Such notions are far from what we've learned about friendship in the past. In the ancient world, friendships were honored across cultures in many great works of literature. Long before Damon and Pythias, there was the ancient Near Eastern story of Gilgamesh and Enkidu and the Homeric story of Achilles and Patroclus. There were biblical stories, such as those of David and Jonathan or Ruth and Naomi. Philosophers such as Confucius, Plato, Aristotle, and Cicero all wrote about friendship, as did many later medieval and modern thinkers. What all these diverse authors have in common is the sense that friendship points to something transcendent in human experience, something that is irreplaceable if we ultimately come to know ourselves and our gifts. What challenges us is the centuries-old belief that a true friendship is a clue to the very meaning of life itself, so much that the prospect of a friend's death is like losing half of oneself. Can we even imagine so profound a meditation on life today?

We talk a lot about sex and romance, and we spend a massive amount of time and money on entertainment, personal care, recreation, and so on, in the belief that a good love life is the key to happiness. We talk less about friendship, even though many ancients believed that friendship was far more central to the good life. It is interesting to ask, for example, whether our rather dismal attitudes toward marriage today signify a suspicion about romance or a failure in cultivating friendship. By many accounts, we are having more romances and more sex; but it is unclear if we are any happier in the end.

Perhaps the issue is that in the twenty-first century, we have become cynical about the possibility of finding real meaning in our lives. We live in the wake of great wars and genocide; we've seen the effect of grasping competition on local and global economies; we've heard the horrific stories of catastrophes, natural and man-made; we've witnessed the toxic effects of false relationships in our lives, in our families, in our workplaces, in our religious communities.

Perhaps the weakness of our friendships today is a result of a timidity in the face of meaning making, such that the "friend" today becomes little more than the person with whom we share sex, or money making, or other small pursuits. We are terrified of being vulnerable, which is the prerequisite for any real relationship, and so we settle for sharing things that advance our social status. When we fall prey to this fear, though, we lose a robust, deep, life-shaping pursuit of love, as far from empty sentimentality as a banquet is from a piece of candy. I am reminded of a haunting observation made by Viktor Frankl, the psychotherapist and Holocaust survivor we met in chapter 3. Reflecting on what distinguished those who survived the camps from those who did not, he described the ones who gave up on meaning as turning away from cultivating any sort of inner life, turning instead to simple pleasures. Later, Frankl described this "existential vacuum" of a person who lacked any will to create meaning in his life:

> Sometimes the frustrated will to meaning is vicariously compensated for by a will to power, including the most primitive form of

the will to power, the will to money. In other cases, the place of frustrated will to meaning is taken by the will to pleasure. That is why existential frustration often eventuates in sexual compensation. We can observe in such cases that the sexual libido becomes rampant in the existential vacuum.

Frankl came to understand a conviction that was shared by poets, philosophers, orators, artists, and thinkers across the ages: namely, that love—and especially in the experience of friendship—is not an end in itself but rather is the result of a greater meaning-making end. To put it more simply, friends emerge not because they seek to be friends with each other but because they discover each other while on a pilgrimage toward something great. Friendship is the by-product of a spiritual search. The corollary to this thesis is that many experiences we call "friendship" today are rather shadows of this most real spiritual journey. These friendships share many of the elements of real friendship: sharing, honesty (to a greater or lesser extent), cooperation, and so on. And for that reason, they will last, often many years. But real friends, as described by the philosophers of old, cannot imagine parting ways because of job transitions, financial woes, tragedies, or growing disinterest—for if they are on a shared pilgrimage, they see the other as a necessary partner.

Of course it is impossible to cultivate deep friendships with everyone. Nevertheless, it is possible to see the seed of real friendship in others and thereby open oneself to the possibility of being a friend. The possibility, suggest the sages, is itself the compass point for a happy life. Perhaps it is even the compass point for finding God.

> *Do I make time to be present with my friend?*
> *What are the concrete ways that my friend knows I value*
>   *him or her?*

SEXUAL DESIRES

Our desire for authentic friendship can also help us discern meaning in our sexual desires. Without this reference point, experiences of sexual desire can feel spontaneous and pointless. They can be seen as cravings when what our souls really yearn for goes unfulfilled.

Sexual desires arise from perfectly normal experiences of life—and this is true whether one is an avowed celibate, a married man or woman, or a single person who longs for a partner or is content to stay single. They are flare-ups of what the writer Ronald Rolheiser calls "divine fire," reflecting on ancient understandings of the primordial and archetypal nature of sexuality. Sexual passion, in some ancient mythologies, led the gods to give birth to the world—it drew lovers into frenzy or competition, sometimes yielding jealousy and even violence and war. The ancients had a strong sensibility about what was at stake in sexual urges because of their connection to life giving: the call to be fruitful was a participation in something holy. Yet they were also very aware that sexuality was caught up in a darker, potentially destructive dimension of human experience, one that had to be tamed by a disciplined will.

Today, we live within an entirely different understanding of sexuality. A host of factors have changed the way we discern meaning in sexual desires. First, the economic order that emerged in the wake of the Industrial Revolution affected views of marriage. Unlike in agricultural or other land-rooted societies, urban societies were not dependent on the cycle of seasons or the necessity to work the land, and people waited longer to get married. The age of first marriage has since risen, meaning that young people experience a longer period of singleness and therefore of sexual desire untethered to a vowed relationship.

Second, our culture has changed how it thinks about sexuality, driven in large part by modern technologies and communications.

As early as the late nineteenth century, advertisers began to understand the effectiveness of manipulating sexual desires to leverage purchasing. Early ads for tobacco and soap included erotic images that had nothing to do with the product sold, but competitors noted that sales often correlated with sexualized advertising. We are now several generations down the road from those early insights; sexual imagery is pervasive and powerfully mimetic. It has an impact on every form of communications media, from magazines in grocery store lines to billboards, TV, film, music, and the Internet. And it has a strong influence on young people, as we saw in the studies by Anne Becker in chapter 1.

> *Over the past day or two, where have you seen attempts to manipulate or elicit sexual desire?*
> *In what ways are your ideas about sex influenced by what you see in movies, TV, advertising, or some other media?*
> *When have you most fully experienced sexual desire as life giving? How was it reflective of who you are now and of the kind of person you want to become?*
> *How might your experiences of sexual desire be a gift to another person? How might they encourage a deepening of relationship with another?*

Third, with new forms of contraception, there is now a strong perception that sex can be kept safely under control by severing the link to procreation. Whereas the ancients could observe patterns of sexual desire related to the natural cycles of the seasons that affected plants, animals, and people, we treat our sexuality the way we treat our lifestyles, as things we control and manipulate at will. And our sexual consumption ends up reflecting other patterns of consumption, with similar results: we overconsume and are left unsatisfied.

Technologized sex has made many of us more likely to act on false desires, as we're impatient to let relationships slowly bloom into mature, life-giving marriages. Which is why in the age of the sexual revolution, we see increasing desires for pornography and sexual behavior at the same time as increased loneliness and a decreasing desire to marry or stay married. The prophet Isaiah's question is poignant: "Why do you spend your money for that which is not bread, and your labor for that which does not satisfy?" (55:2). When sex is disconnected from the meaning it gains in a deepening, life-long friendship, it becomes unsatisfying.

In recent years, more and more literature has underscored that observation, especially among young people. Consider the titles as a clue to what researchers are discovering: *Unhooked: How Young Women Pursue Sex, Delay Love and Lose at Both; Guyland: The Perilous World Where Boys Become Men; Girls Uncovered: New Research on What America's Sexual Culture Does to Young Women; The End of Sex: How Hookup Culture Is Leaving a Generation Unhappy, Sexually Unfulfilled, and Confused about Intimacy.* One author tells a story of a beautiful young college student who works as a model and laments a campus culture in which sex is the norm and dating does not exist. She must play a relationship game whose rules no one understands, a game most people don't really like and that turns a normal, healthy desire for relationship into a compulsive shopping for hookups. Both men and women are subject to what sociologists call "pluralistic ignorance"—that is, the sense that everyone else is having more fun—even though the data suggest that the social dynamics are often toxic for forming real romantic friendships.

It is possible to come to understand one's experience of sexual desires in the context of a larger pyramid of good desires that help us discern our life's meaning. Discernment of all desires is a key to knowing God, the author of our lives. Sexual desires are no different:

through discernment, we come to understand them as not influenced by unhealthy or manipulative social pressures but as part of the integrated persons God has created us to be, in relationship to others, called to be mirrors of divine love.

It is certainly the task of every mature person to grasp the meaning and vocation in their lives so that they can discern how to integrate their sexual desires. For some, that integration will be fruitful celibacy, that is, a celibacy that enters authentically into intimate friendships. For others, that integration will involve periods of discerning relationships, seeking a partner for whom they are a gift and who in turn is a gift to them. Ultimately, many are called to a fruitful marriage: a sacramental friendship that is a sign of the kingdom of God. In every case, though, the goal is the integration of sexual desire into a life imbued with meaning and purpose.

FRIENDSHIP AND BEAUTY

We come to see the world in its beauty through the eyes of a friend. We come to understand our heart's capacity to love—a capacity that the philosopher Blaise Pascal hints at in his comment that the heart has its reasons that reason does not know. For in beginning to practice friendship love, we discover both something about who God has created us to be, capable of being a grace to another person, and something about the world in its wonder. We no longer live only for ourselves but for the other, and as a result we find that new dimensions of meaning open up. For what gives us joy is no longer only the satisfaction of our desire; it is also that which satisfies the desire of our friend and through whose joy we too experience joy.

Nowhere do I find a more profound exploration of these dimensions of meaning than in the meditative poem "In Memoriam A.H.H.," by Alfred, Lord Tennyson. Written more than seventeen years after the death of his college friend, Arthur Henry Hallam, the poem not only praises who Hallam was as a friend but also explores the way that friendship opened Tennyson's eyes to the meaning of life and the soul's capacity for love. Tennyson was writing just before the publication of Charles Darwin's *Origin of Species*, which raised questions about the age of the earth and the way that God was involved in creation. Tennyson himself writes of the way that Hallam's death challenged his understanding of providence but also of how his experience of grief changed the way he saw his soul's participation in a world created by a loving God. Addressing the Son of God the way an ancient poet might have addressed the Muses, he writes:

> Thine are these orbs of light and shade;
> Thou madest Life in man and brute;
> Thou madest Death; and lo, thy foot
> Is on the skull which thou hast made.

For Tennyson, God is the one who has made a world in which there is both light and darkness, life and death. We are all destined for death, but we are also capable of understanding the meaning of life and death in ways that tap into God's own wisdom. Our ways of understanding are "but broken lights of thee," which may grow to be more like God by contemplating reverently the light of God. Tennyson confesses that his friendship with Hallam was, in life, and remains, in death, a mode of such contemplation: "I trust he lives in thee, and there / I find him worthier to be loved."

His grief is painful—he sees places all around him that bring back memories of his friend. He draws comparisons between the meaning of his friendship and the experiences of other forms of love. Yet twice he returns to a couplet that has since entered into common parlance: "'Tis better to have loved and lost / Than never to have loved at all." For Tennyson, the experience of loving a friend opened him to a new understanding of the meaning of life, even though it also opened him up to a more profound understanding of death.

One person who was deeply moved by Tennyson's meditation was Queen Victoria, for whom the poem was a great comfort after the death of her husband Prince Albert. In an album that was a kind of writing therapy, she copied and underlined several lines that underscored what her marriage to Albert had meant to her:

I know that this was Life,—the track
Whereon with equal feet we fared;
And then, as now, the day prepared
The daily burden for the back.

But this it was that made me move
As light as carrier-birds in air;
I loved the weight I had to bear,
Because it needed help of Love:

Nor could I weary, heart or limb,
When mighty Love would cleave in twain
The lading of a single pain,
And part it, giving half to him.

One can imagine the queen remembering the way her husband had shared her burdens, "cleav[ing] in twain" the pain that she bore as a head of state. It must have been lonely to hold the power she did. But she, unlike the tyrant Dionysius, was wise enough to know that authentic friendship can make the weight of life as "light as carrier-birds in air."

The most foundational of our desires is the desire to love and to be loved. That foundational desire is, I think, a clue to what the ancient Israelites meant by describing the human being as made in the image and likeness of God. Human beings crave intimacy, but too often we substitute diminished forms of relationship that do not satisfy our cravings. True friendship—a sharing of hearts in a pilgrimage toward the good, the true, and the beautiful—is a taste of heaven. Even grief, the loss of a heart's desire, is its mirror image, for only a heart capable of love is capable of grief. The heart that experiences grief is, if we follow Tennyson's logic, still better off than the one that has never loved at all, for at least it knows clearly what it desires. It has encountered something of God, and it will mature through the grieving process, even as it continues to feel the loss of the beloved. It will, in time, remember that lost love is proof of one's ability to love, and will, with Tennyson himself, recall that it is therefore possible to love again:

> My heart, tho' widow'd, may not rest
> Quite in the love of what is gone,
> But seeks to beat in time with one
> That warms another living breast.

The death of a friend is thus not the end of one's pilgrimage through life; it is rather an interruption. The important thing is to once again resume walking, resume loving, and remember how the love of a friend is a window to God.

NEXT STEPS:

1. Think about someone who has journeyed with you through a certain stage in your life and helped you get where you needed to go. What were the characteristics of that relationship? How did that relationship make you feel?

2. Bring to mind a relationship that did not feel authentic. What were the characteristics that made it feel inauthentic? What feelings did it stir up in you? What is the state of that relationship now?

3. Think about how you interact with friends on social media. What are one or two ways you can use social media to build real and lasting friendships?

7

SERVE OTHERS

It is above all a question of interdependence. . . . This then is not a feeling of vague compassion or shallow distress at the misfortunes of so many people, both near and far. On the contrary, it is a firm and persevering determination to commit oneself to the common good; that is to say to the good of all and of each individual, because we are all really responsible for all.
—St. John Paul II, *Sollicitudo Rei Socialis*, 1987

At a time when we can know so much about cultures around the world, we have become more alienated from one another than ever before. Before the Internet, our knowledge about our society and other cultures was primarily through books or TV. Now, when instant knowledge of events across the globe is at our fingertips, there is a change in the way people try to understand other cultures. Less frequently do we rely on authorities to tell us about the world, be it a TV news network or a well-respected travel guide. We have become our own networking hubs, piecing together information that we glean, often haphazardly, from the web. We retreat into like-minded social networks, such that our news feeds become exercises in confirmation bias, with friends sharing stories that reinforce opinions about others that we already share. Instead of bringing the world closer together, our virtual networks often drive people farther and farther apart—even when the dividing lines run through the same neighborhoods and cities.

Why have we become more alienated? Why is it that, in the United States—a country built on the hope that people from different cultures could live together under one system of government—there have been new, virulent strains of racism and classism? Why, in a world that knows how to eradicate poverty, do we see powerful political and economic forces consolidate wealth rather than expand its growth, especially to those in desperate situations of need? Why are so many children denied life, either killed *in utero* or starved in infancy? Why is there such prevalence of violence against women? Why do so many people lack access to clean water or adequate sanitation? These and many other serious problems point to the ways our communities fail to live in solidarity. For, all of these problems are rooted in a failure to see others as another self, another person worthy of the same love that every soul craves. The consequence of this failure is to see others as burdens or enemies to be overcome through political machinations or violence.

An authentic life is one that acknowledges the difficult, often strained relationships that exist among people today. One cannot hide one's head in the sand, pretending that a general commitment to being a good person is sufficient. One can lead a reflective life; seek graced understanding of oneself and one's experiences; live with a sense of purpose, seeking out kinship and being an authentic friend to others. But, to paraphrase St. Paul, if one does not take the extra step of coming to understand one's place among fellow citizens, one is a clashing cymbal: "If I speak in the tongues of mortals and of angels, but do not have love, I am a noisy gong or a clanging cymbal." (1 Corinthians 13:1)

The direction of an authentic life is always one that serves others. It may be a life of contemplative prayer in a cloister, in a service profession, parenting, or entrepreneurship that lifts people out of poverty. It may be solitary or familial. It may be some kind of engagement in politics or social activism. It may be in medicine, academia, business, entertainment, public service, law, or any number of other fields. But in the end, living authentically, to quote St. John Paul II, is a question of interdependence, of committing oneself to the common good. It is, in its most basic reality, a question of a person coming to understand that one's good is intimately tied to the good of everyone else and that an authentic life is one that embraces a responsibility toward the society of which one is a small part—including those who agree with you and, especially, those who do not. It is to love one's neighbors even when they are enemies—for doing so is, if we follow the ancients, a taste of the divine.

LEARNING FROM THE ANCIENT WORLD

Good ideas tend to hang around for a long time, particularly when they are as basic as how to get along with one another. Ancient wisdom, I am convinced, can help us understand the roots of our alienation from one another and point us toward more authentic, shared lives.

Throughout time, people have always tended to identify closely with and pledge their allegiance to a family, tribe, or local group. History is rife with examples of tribal warfare. In ancient history, however, a more expansive view of citizenship emerged, one that was rooted in beliefs that the gods demanded care for others. There is a certain intuitive logic here: the impulse to broaden one's care of others beyond one's immediate family or nation draws one nearer to the divine, to an ethic of care that has no boundaries.

In the ancient Near East, Greece, and Rome, when war was as much a reality as growing food and raising a family, a primitive religious belief in being hospitable to strangers nevertheless developed. In Homer's *Iliad* and *Odyssey*, there are many examples of the practice of *xenia*, or hospitality toward strangers and even enemies.

The *Iliad* is a story that begins with a prince named Paris, who violates xenia when he steals the wife, Helen, of his host Menelaus. In response, Menelaus and his brother launch an army to sack Paris's home, the city of Troy. In the midst of this Trojan War, there is a striking story of two warriors, Glaukos and Diomedes, meeting on the battlefield to do battle. They exchange stories of who they are and where they come from. But when Glaukos narrates that he is the son of Bellerophon, Diomedes plants his spear in the ground and pledges that they will not fight, for his own grandfather was a friend to Bellerophon. The imperative of xenia interrupts even the heat of the Trojan War.

In the *Odyssey*, xenia is a theme throughout the story. Odysseus, who has been at war for ten years, spends ten more trying to return home. In the meantime, many suitors seek the hand of his wife Penelope, pressing her to declare once and for all that her husband has died. But as she demurs, they grossly violate the norms of xenia, despoiling Odysseus's estate. In another strand of the story, Odysseus and his men find themselves stranded on the island where Polyphemus, the Cyclops, lives. He too places himself above the gods by trampling the norms of xenia, attacking the men and trying to eat them. In both of these cases, those who violate xenia ultimately pay a price for their disregard for the law of the gods. In contrast, there are several stories of the proper exercise of xenia, such as when Telemachus, Odysseus's son, visits the kings Nestor and Menelaus, or when Nausicaä hosts Odysseus in her home. Xenia is the virtue of embracing friends and strangers as though they might be messengers from the gods. Indeed, the very name *Zeus Xenios* points to hospitality as being protected by the ruler of the gods.

The Old Testament story of Abraham welcoming angels is about a similar theme. Abraham meets three men near a great tree and shows them reverence and hospitality, enjoining his wife, Sarah, to make three cakes for them. They receive his hospitality, and then prophesize that within the year, Sarah, advanced in age, will bear a son. Later, there is the story of Elijah and the widow of Zarephath, who is gathering sticks to make what she fears will be a final meal for herself and her son before a famine leads to their starvation. Elijah enjoins her to make him a cake, and as long as he stays with her she does not run out of food. (1 Kings 17:7–16) Elsewhere, in the Torah, the command to welcome the stranger is repeated thirty-five times, more than any other command, for the Lord says to Israel, "You too were once a stranger in the land of Egypt." Similar stories pervade ancient literature.

Jesus broadened the imperative of hospitality by calling his followers to love their enemies and pray for those who persecute them. Jesus' logic is simple: just as the Father welcomes sinners into a relationship, so we should reach out to our enemies and draw them into relationship. Jesus illustrates this in his reaching out to foreigners such as the Samaritan woman and the Roman centurion.

The earliest Christian communities similarly sought to practice xenia. Jesus called Paul to a *koinonia*, or "communion," a spiritual and moral union of souls ordered together toward God. Koinonia is Paul's preferred way to describe the relationships among early Christians and between Christians and Christ himself. The earliest Christians dedicated themselves to prayer and fellowship; Paul exhorted the churches in far off cities to make contributions to support the saints in Jerusalem; Christians were called to fellowship with Christ and to participate in sharing his body and blood. What Paul had in mind was a relationship among believers that mirrors the intimate union of the Father, the Son, and the Holy Spirit. "Let the same mind be in you that was in Christ Jesus, who, though he was in the form of God, did not regard equality with God as something to be exploited," he wrote. (Philippians 2:5–6) The attitude of the

Christian, in other words, was to love both friends and enemies alike. (Matthew 5:43–48) Elsewhere Paul refers to the "communion of the Holy Spirit" being the goal of the Christian community. (2 Corinthians 13:13) John, similarly, summons the early Christians to fellowship with one another by first having fellowship with God himself: "we declare to you what we have seen and heard so that you also may have fellowship with us; and truly our fellowship is with the Father and with his Son Jesus Christ." (1 John 1:3)

For Paul, the society that Jesus called for was a clear rejection of tribalism or nationalism. For the Christian life was not to be understood as a kind of withdrawal into a cult isolated from the rest of the world. On the contrary, the Christian life meant becoming "citizens with the saints and also members of the household of God" (Ephesians 2:19) within the existing structures of rule in the Roman Empire and beyond. He calls for a new moral order within the human heart itself—a turning away from the moral cul-de-sac of selfish desires and toward an expansive love of others. What gives us life, he suggests, is living in imitation of the love of God and working to transform existing societies from within.

GOD'S INVITATION

Every human being faces a fundamental choice of how to live, whether ultimately for oneself or for others. The choice to live for others—to love—is already a participation in the life of God. In the language of the ancient hymn, "Ubi caritas et amor, Deus ibi est," where there is self-giving and love, God is there. We share in God's life when we respond to love's call.

Andrei Rublev (public domain), via Wikipedia Commons

Perhaps the best-known image of this invitation to love is the icon of the Holy Trinity written by Andrei Rublev in early fifteenth-century Russia. His depiction of the three angels that Abraham hosted not only calls to mind the Christian doctrine of God-in-three-persons—Father, Son, and Holy Spirit—but also signifies a call to enter into koinonia with God and so share in the life of self-giving love that is the reality of the divine life. The icon tilts, as it were, toward the viewer, with an open-ended table pointing out from the three angels, inviting the viewer to sit at the table. The angel at the left represents the Father, with the other two looking toward him; the Father gazes toward the Son on the right and raises his hand in a gesture of peace. He *sees* the Son.

The icon is an invitation to "act in God's eye." After all, in God's eye we are the image of Christ, the Word of God enfleshed. We are invited into the koinonia of the Trinity as we are, in order that through the Holy Spirit we might manifest God's Word in the world. By doing so, we answer the Father's invitation to each creature to become itself—to selve—by entering into the life of the Trinity. "He has given us . . . his precious and very great promises, so that through them you may . . . become participants of the divine nature," wrote the author of the second letter of Peter (1:4). What this means is that God's invitation is to be what God has created us to be and thereby to gain a piece of heaven. I must be myself; you must be yourself, and no other.

The implication of this koinonia theology is that we come to realize the full reality of who we are within the human family. That reality is always concrete: it is earning money, buying food, raising children, paying taxes, taking care of a home. It is listening to leaders in government and asking how the laws they make will serve the poor. It is asking hard questions about who has access to the goods of the earth and who has been shut out. It is paying attention to the ways that disparity can breed desperation and even violence. It is seeking to understand the gang member in Los Angeles and the subsistence farmer in El Salvador. It is remembering Jesus' lament to his disciples:

> Then the king will say to those at his right hand, "Come, you that are blessed by my Father, inherit the kingdom prepared for you from the foundation of the world; for I was hungry and you gave me food, I was thirsty and you gave me something to drink, I was a stranger and you welcomed me, I was naked and you gave me

clothing, I was sick and you took care of me, I was in prison and you visited me." Then the righteous will answer him, "Lord, when was it that we saw you hungry and gave you food, or thirsty and gave you something to drink? And when was it that we saw you a stranger and welcomed you, or naked and gave you clothing? And when was it that we saw you sick or in prison and visited you?" And the king will answer them, "Truly I tell you, just as you did it to one of the least of these who are members of my family, you did it to me."

—Matthew 25:34–40

St. Ignatius offers an image of God "laboring" in creation and of Christ the King calling the devout soul to labor with him in the work of redemption. God's invitation is to be part of that laboring, helping to bring about a taste of the heavenly kingdom by being Christ in the world.

> *Whom do you feel called to serve?*
> *Whom have you served lately?*
> *How have you shown hospitality to another recently?*
> *How did you feel after?*
> *What experiences of service to others have had an impact on you?*
> *Do you discern a desire to serve others in a particular way? What are you doing about it?*

OUR CITIZENSHIP

An image that Jesus uses in the Gospels to describe the kingdom of God is that of yeast or leaven: "The kingdom of heaven is like yeast that a woman took and mixed in with three measures of flour until all of it was leavened." (Matthew 13:33) Three measures was a vast amount, enough to feed a hundred people. Jesus' hyperbole points to the image as encompassing all people—the yeast becomes *katholikos*, catholic, the Greek word meaning "throughout the whole" of the batch. Walter Ong, a Jesuit priest and language scholar, suggests an important distinction in understanding this parable: the yeast is not "universal," a word suggesting that it turns the batch into itself. Rather, the yeast is "catholic," a word suggesting the opposite: that the yeast dies and transforms the batch into bread. The yeast makes the bread what it most truly is.

For the Christian, citizenship in the kingdom of heaven means being willing to be yeast. It means being catholic, in the sense of being willing to allow oneself to bring the world into the full reality of what it is. It is neither denial of one's own being nor a demand that others deny who they are; it is the willingness to be transformed as one enters into the world to transform it. Our citizenship in the kingdom of God does not absolve us from citizenship in the communities or nations where we live; on the contrary, it demands our willingness to transform those communities into places where all share in the common good.

In his encyclical *Laudato Si'*, Pope Francis describes the challenge of seeking the common good amid a broken world. He points to the creation stories in the book of Genesis and highlights the biblical view of creation as a window to understanding our current challenges:

> The creation accounts in the book of Genesis . . . suggest that human life is grounded in three fundamental and closely intertwined relationships: with God, with our neighbour and with the earth itself. According to the Bible, these three vital relationships have been broken, both outwardly and within us. This rupture is sin.

Like his predecessors, Pope Francis seeks to apply this and other biblical insights to contemporary problems, considering challenges to the common good through the lens of Catholic social teaching. For him, sin manifests itself in a disordered society: it twists relationships and skews our perception of the world so that we can no longer see the way that the world might regain the original justice with which God created it. The citizen of the kingdom, then, is one who is willing to take a long, loving look at injustice, not only asking how the world is now but also imagining how it might be if it were more just. Not only that: the citizen acts toward what he or she imagines, embodying in his or her very life the justice desired by God. The just person justices. The just person keeps grace, the free gift of God's love, by passing along the gifts that he or she has received.

TEN THOUSAND PLACES

A scan of the news can be discouraging, causing us to wonder where God is when there is so much pain. For many, the response to this pain is withdrawal, by looking past those who sting our consciences. But the central symbol of Christian faith is the cross: the focal point of God's willingness to lean into the suffering of the world. For philosopher René Girard, God's willingness to enter into the violence of the world and take it upon himself is the central mystery that defines Christian faith and distances it from primitive religion. Rather than require a sacrifice to satiate the divine anger, Christ enters human history in order to become the sacrifice that transforms the world. We who are conformed to Christ similarly enter into the messiness of the world like yeast in order to transform it.

What that means is that each and every person on the earth has been created for a purpose—to be Christ in ten thousand places, transforming the world through love. In the end, discernment is the practice of listening for the ways that you might fulfill God's purpose in creating you to do some good in the world. I am reminded of the beautiful meditation by John Henry Newman:

God has created me to do Him some definite service; He has committed some work to me which He has not committed to another. I have my mission—I never may know it in this life, but I shall be told it in the next. Somehow I am necessary for His purposes, as necessary in my place as an Archangel in his—if, indeed, I fail, He can raise another, as He could make the stones children of Abraham. Yet I have a part in this great work; I am a link in a chain, a bond of connexion between persons. He has not created me for naught. I shall do good, I shall do His work; I shall be an angel of peace, a preacher of truth in my own place, while not intending it, if I do but keep His commandments and serve Him in my calling.

Therefore I will trust Him. Whatever, wherever I am, I can never be thrown away. If I am in sickness, my sickness may serve Him; in perplexity, my perplexity may serve Him; if I am in sorrow, my sorrow may serve Him. My sickness, or perplexity, or sorrow may be necessary causes of some great end, which is quite beyond us. He does nothing in vain; He may prolong my life, He may shorten it; He knows what He is about. He may take away my friends, He may throw me among strangers, He may make me feel desolate, make my spirits sink, hide the future from me—still He knows what He is about.

I pray with this meditation often, especially in times when it seems that I am hamstrung by mistakes and sins. God's creativity is greater than my failures, and God's desire for the world is great enough to inspire anyone, no matter how unlikely, to serve the good God seeks to do in the world.

Living against the grain of the world means rejecting anything that is false or partially true, in favor of an expansive, creative, world-affirming truth—a truth that all of us human beings, from the moment of our conception until the moment when the Lord calls us home, have a mission, a purpose, a capacity to be both the object of love and a human subject with whom others can enter into loving relationship. Even those who are very young, very old, sick, or disabled, whom the world may not see as persons worthy of care, are creatures of a loving God—creatures for whom you may exercise care and attention, whose very existence summons from us new modes of gifts. The grain of the world runs toward the useful, the profitable, the convenient, the entertaining, the ephemeral. The grain of the kingdom runs toward the beautiful, the sacrificial, the truthful, the mystagogical, the eternal. The prayer of discernment is the prayer that we should always desire to live with the grain of the kingdom. The promise of discernment is that in doing so, we will find those who will grow with us in holiness—another way of saying that like us, they will desire to be their most authentic selves.

NEXT STEPS:

1. From the desires you've identified about yourself throughout this book, in what ways do you see yourself serving others? Jot down a few ideas.

2. What does it mean to you to be "catholic"? Identify one of the changes you'd like to make to live a more authentic, catholic life.

3. Bring to mind a time when you were hospitable to another person. What did you do? How did you serve him or her? What feelings did it bring about in you? Now identify a time when someone was hospitable to you. How did he or she serve you? What did this person say? How did it make you feel? List five ways that you can show hospitality to a person that fits in with your life now and what you have to offer. Pick one and try to think about how you'll act on it.

4. What have you learned about yourself while journeying with this book? Sketch out two or three actions you'll take based on

who you are, the desires God has given you, and the opportunities that you have right now.

ACKNOWLEDGMENTS

I'm thankful for the encouragement of many people before and during the writing process. First, my many students over the years, both at Mount Aloysius College and Boston College, whose willingness to share their stories has inspired me. The fact that many former students still e-mail and visit to talk about their discernment process is not only personally enriching but also professionally informative, as it has given me a long view of what Ignatian discernment looks like in real life. If you are one of my alumni, don't be a stranger! Find me on Facebook at facebook.com/muldoont.

Second, I'm grateful to colleagues in the Capstone program at Boston College, and especially Professor Jim Weiss of the Department of Theology, the longtime chair of the program. I'm also grateful to colleagues in the Honors Program, whose reading of classic texts in the Western tradition has deepened my understanding of the roots of modernity. My teaching has been enriched by learning from others who not only root themselves in Ignatian spirituality but also share insights gained from deep, sustained immersion in different disciplines.

Third, I am thankful for friends at Loyola Press, especially Joe Durepos, with whom I first hatched the idea of this, my fourth book with the Press, as well as Becca Russo and Vinita Wright. Finally, I'm grateful to Rosemary Lane for her very careful read of the manuscript and suggestions on how to make a rather academic book much more appealing to readers.

ADDITIONAL READING

Herbert Alphonso, SJ. *Discovering Your Personal Vocation.* New York: Paulist Press, 2001.

George Aschenbrenner, SJ. *Consciousness Examen.* Chicago: Loyola Press, 2007.

Greg Boyle. *Tattoos on the Heart: The Power of Boundless Compassion.* New York: Free Press, 2011.

Dean Brackley, SJ. *The Call to Discernment in Troubled Times.* New York: Crossroad Publishing, 2005.

Viktor Frankl. *Man's Search for Meaning* (many editions).

Timothy Gallagher, OMV. *Discerning the Will of God: An Ignatian Guide to Christian Decision Making.* New York: Crossroad Publishing, 2009.

Timothy Gallagher, OMV. *Discernment of Spirits: An Ignatian Guide for Everyday Living.* New York: Crossroad Publishing, 2005.

Dennis Hamm, SJ. "Rummaging for God: Praying Backwards through Your Day," *America*, May 14, 1994, republished at IgnatianSpirituality.com, www.ignatianspirituality.com/ ignatian-prayer/the-examen/ rummaging-for-god-praying-backward-through-your-day.

Christopher Jamison. *Finding Happiness: Monastic Steps for a Fulfilling Life.* Collegeville, MN: Liturgical Press, 2008.

Christopher Kaczor. *The Gospel of Happiness.* New York: Image
    Books, 2015.

James Martin, SJ. *The Jesuit Guide to (Almost) Everything.* San
    Francisco: HarperOne, 2012.

Henri Nouwen, with Michael J. Christensen and Rebecca J. Laird.
    Discernment: Reading the Signs of Daily Life. San Francisco:
    HarperOne, 2013.

Mark E. Thibodeaux, SJ. *Reimagining the Ignatian Examen.*
    Chicago: Loyola Press, 2015.

Jean Vanier. *Becoming Human,* 10th anniversary ed. Mahwah, NJ:
    Paulist Press, 2008.

ENDNOTES

Page x: **"A long, loving look at the real"** Walter Burghardt, SJ, "A Long, Loving Look at the Real," reprinted in George S. Traub, SJ, ed., *The Ignatian Spirituality Reader* (Chicago: Loyola Press, 2008), 89–98.

Page xii: **St. Augustine's autobiography** *Confessions* Augustine, *Confessions*, trans. Henry Chadwick (Oxford University Press, 2008), IV.iv.9.

Page xiv: **"More intimate to me than I am to myself"** Augustine, *Confessions*, III.vi.11, my translation.

Page xv: **In Peter's second letter, he points to these promises** This text exemplifies the Christian doctrine of *theosis*, or deification.

Page xv: **The great philosopher Martin Buber** Martin Buber, *Tales of the Hassidim: The Early Masters* (New York: Schocken Books, 1968), 141.

Page xv: **Similarly, the poet Rumi wrote about** Rumi, "Say Yes Quickly," *Open Secret*, trans. Coleman Barks (Putney, VT: Threshold Books, 1984), 69.

Page 1: **You have been thrown into the world** I borrow from Heidegger's notion of *Geworfenheit* ("throwness") here. See his *Being and Time* (New York: Harper Perennial Modern Classics, 2008), division 1, chapter 5.

Page 2: **Imitation, or mimesis (as Aristotle called it)** I use Aristotle's understanding as evident in the *Poetics*, rather than Plato's idea that mimesis is twice removed from reality. I am interested in the way Aristotle sees mimesis as a meaning-making function in drama. This basic dynamic—that is, of the human capacity for meaning making through engagement in a story—is fundamental to the *Spiritual Exercises* of St. Ignatius of Loyola. In what follows, I am also influenced by the work of René Girard.

Page 2: **As Mary Oliver wrote: Tell me, what is it you plan to do** Mary Oliver, "The Summer Day," from *New and Selected Poems* (Boston: Beacon Press, 1992).

Page 3: "Outside the walls of the Circle, all was noise" Dave Eggers, *The Circle* (New York: Alfred A. Knopf and McSweeney's Books, 2013), 31.

Page 4: "I mean, all this stuff you're involved in, it's all gossip" Ibid., 133.

Page 4: "Now all humans will have the eyes of God" Ibid., 398–99.

Page 6: According to the Pew Research Center, 92 percent of teens Pew Research Center, "Teens, Social Media & Technology Overview 2015," http://www.pewinternet.org/2015/04/09/teens-social-media-technology-2015/.

Page 6: Since adolescence is a period when See Kimberly Leonard, "Is Social Media Making Self-Harm Worse for Teens?," *US News and World Report*, May 29, 2015, http://www.usnews.com/news/articles/2015/05/29/ is-social-media-making-self-harm-worse-for-teens; Stephanie Pappas, "Cyberbullying on Social Media Linked to Teen Depression," Fox News, June 25, 2015, http://foxnews.com/health/2015/06/23/ cyberbullying-on-social-media-linked-to-teen-depression/; and Tim Elmore, "Nomophobia: A Rising Trend in Students," *Psychology Today*, September 18, 2014, https://www.psychologytoday.com/blog/artificial-maturity/201409/ nomophobia-rising-trend-in-students.

Page 6: Anne Becker, a researcher at Harvard Medical School For a good summary of Becker's work, see "Study Examines Link between Media Consumption, Eating Disorders, among Adolescent Girls in Fiji," News, AZO Network, January 7, 2011, http://www.news-medical.net/news/20110107/ Study-examines-link-between-media-consumption-eating-disorders-among-adolescent-girls-in-Fiji.aspx.

Page 8: Deborah Serani, a psychologist and author of the award-winning book Deborah Serani, cited in Alice G. Walton, "Why the Super-Successful Get Depressed," *Forbes*, January 26, 2015.

Page 8: We are constantly comparing ourselves to others Alina Tugend, in "Comparing Yourself to Others: It's Not All Bad" (*New York Times*, July 1, 2011), summarizes several studies that point to mimetic rivalry in its classic American form of keeping up with the Joneses. One such study, "Neighbors as Negatives: Relative Earnings and Well-Being," published in 2005 in *Quarterly Journal of Economics*, found that "higher earnings of neighbors were associated with lower levels of self-reported happiness." Later: "If you can't change what you did, then downward social comparison helps us gain perspective. And those people are able to move on and re-engage in other goals. If you compare upward about things you can't change, then you seem to just feel stuck."

Page 8: Here is how the journalist Shane Snow puts it Shane Snow, "The Fascinating Reason Many Billionaires Get Depressed (and How They Snap Out of It)," *Business Insider*, September 26, 2014, http://www.businessinsider.com/psychology-of-success-why-billionaires-get-depressed-2014-9.

Page 10: Radically different from sitting in a cubicle, for example See Sarah Green Carmichael, "Why Cubicles Are the Worst," *Harvard Business Review*, November 13, 2013, https://hbr.org/2013/11/research-cubicles-are-the-absolute-worst.

Page 10: Doctors are emphasizing how physical exercise can dramatically improve mental health See John J. Ratey, *Spark: The Revolutionary New Science of Exercise and the Brain* (New York: Little, Brown, 2008).

Page 11: Our dependence upon one another, our common home I am drawing from the beautiful imagery in Pope Francis's encyclical *Laudato Si'*.

Page 11: "Satisfaction is a lowly / thing, how pure a thing is joy" Marianne Moore, "What Are Years?" in *What Are Years?* (New York: Macmillan, 1941).

Page 11: Researchers who study "captology" See Ian Leslie, "The Scientists Who Make Apps Addictive," *The Economist*, October/November 2016, http://www.1843magazine.com/features/the-scientists-who-make-apps-addictive.

Page 12: In the Gospels, Jesus uses the image of scattered seeds See Mark 4:3–20.

Page 18: We delighted in the early days of parenting My book *Longing to Love* is a memoir of discernment that tells the story of our difficult road to becoming parents (Chicago: Loyola Press, 2010).

Page 18: The technology writer Nicholas Carr points to this phenomenon Nicholas Carr, *The Shallows, What the Internet Is Doing to Our Brains* (New York: W.W. Norton, 2011).

Page 18: Recent neurobiology studies show that we are naturally See Cell Press, "Pure Novelty Spurs the Brain," *ScienceDaily*, August 27, 2006, http://www.sciencedaily.com/releases/2006/08/060826180547.htm.

Page 19: "The endless cycle of idea and action" T. S. Eliot, opening stanza from *Choruses from "The Rock"* (London: Faber and Faber, 1934).

Page 19: By Attending to the Word underneath all words Some of this material is influenced by Karl Rahner's *Hearer of the Word: Laying a Foundation for a Philosophy of Religion*, trans. Joseph Donceel (New York: Bloomsbury Academic, 1994), as well as Thomas Aquinas's treatment of the procession of the inner word (*verbum*) as analyzed by Bernard Lonergan in *Verbum: Word and Idea in Aquinas*, in *Collected Works of Bernard Lonergan*, Vol. 2 (Toronto: University of Toronto Press, 1997).

Page 20: They can lead to inventions that serve humanity I have in mind here the critiques of competition in the sciences as corrosive both to the sciences themselves as well as to larger ecological and moral questions. See, for example, F. C. Fang and A. Casadevall, "Competitive Science: Is Competition Ruining Science?" in *Infection and Immunity* 83, no. 4 (2015): 1229–33. See also Pope Francis's critiques of the "technocratic paradigm," as in *Laudato Si'*, chapter 3, section 2. He writes, "The technocratic paradigm also tends to dominate economic and political life. The economy accepts every advance in technology with a view to profit, without concern for its potentially negative impact on human beings" (109).

Page 21: A living wisdom that moves the sun and the other stars A reference to the closing lines of Dante's *Paradiso*.

Page 23: For what happens in gazing and beholding is an awareness I am indebted in this section to Michael Himes's thesis that Catholic education ought to help students become beholders, in his essay "Living Conversations," *Conversations on Jesuit Higher Education* (1995): 21–27.

Page 23: All of us are vulnerable to various forms of bias Here I am influenced by Bernard Lonergan's notions of bias as explored in *Insight: A Study of Human Understanding* (Toronto: University of Toronto Press, 1992).

Page 24: Socrates once opined that the unexamined life See Plato's *Apology*, 38a. See further, Pierre Hadot, *Philosophy as a Way of Life: Spiritual Exercises from Socrates to Foucault* (Malden, MA: Wiley-Blackwell, 1995).

Page 25: George Aschenbrenner, SJ, describes this practice in a seminal 1972 essay George Aschenbrenner, SJ, *Consciousness Examen* (Chicago: Loyola Press, 2007).

Page 27: "Take, Lord, and receive all my liberty" From *The Spiritual Exercises* 234, in *Ignatius of Loyola: The Spiritual Exercises and Selected Works*, ed. George Ganss, SJ (Mahwah, NJ: Paulist Press, 1991), 177.

Page 27: "Truly the chief exercise in mystical theology" From *Treatise on the Love of God*, trans. Henry Benedict Mackey, OSB (New York: Benziger Brothers, c. 1884), book 6, chap. 1.

Page 29: Colleagues from the Greater Good Science Center at the University of California, Berkeley See the Greater Good Science Center's website at http://greatergood.berkeley.edu, and especially the essay by Robert Emmons,

"Why Gratitude is Good," available at http://greatergood.berkeley.edu/article/item/why_gratitude_is_good/.

Page 31: **Author Dennis Hamm, SJ, uses the image of rummaging** Dennis Hamm, SJ, "Rummaging for God: Praying Backwards through Your Day," *America*, May 14, 1994, republished at http://www.ignatianspirituality.com/ignatian-prayer/the-examen/rummaging-for-god-praying-backward-through-your-day.

Page 35: **Driven by advances in positive psychology** See Christopher Kaczor, *The Gospel of Happiness* (New York: Image Books, 2015), which relies on a number of recent developments in the science of positive psychology.

Page 35: **The seventeenth-century French mathematician and philosopher** Blaise Pascal: *Pensées* (New York: Penguin Classics, 1995), 425.

Page 38: **From Mesopotamia to ancient Greece and India** I am thinking of such works as *Epic of Gilgamesh*, the epics of Homer, and the Vedas, in which gods and mortals interact freely.

Page 38: **In a similar vein, the Talmud has the story of Death** The story is told in Hershey H. Friedman and Linda Weiser Friedman, *God Laughed: Sources of Jewish Humor* (Piscataway, NJ: Transaction Books, 2014).

Page 40: **Viktor Frankl (1905–1997) was an Austrian neurologist** Viktor Frankl, *Man's Search for Meaning* (Boston: Beacon Press, 2006). The following citations from the book are from this version.

Page 41: **"I said that someone looks down on"** Ibid., 83.

Page 41: **"A thought transfixed me: for the first time"** Ibid., 37.

Page 42: **"To the European, it is a characteristic of the American culture"** Frankl is quoted in "The Case for a Tragic Optimism," ibid., 138.

Page 45: **"When he was thinking of those things of the world"** Ignatius of Loyola, from his *Autobiography*, trans. Parmanda R. Divarkar, in *Ignatius of Loyola: Spiritual Exercises and Selected Works*, ed. George Ganss, SJ (New York: Paulist Press, 1991).

Page 46: **Neurochemists, neurobiologists, and neuropsychologists are coming to a greater** See Julie Beck's interview with Rick Hanson of the Greater Good Science Center in "How to Build a Happier Brain," *The Atlantic*, October 13, 2013, www.theatlantic.com/health/archive/2013/10/how-to-build-a-happier-brain/280752/.

Page 46: **Psychologists who study the machinery of memory have found** See Maria Konnikova's article "You Have No Idea What Happened," *New Yorker*, February 4, 2015, http://www.newyorker.com/science/maria-konnikova/ idea-happened-memory-recollection, which focuses on strong emotional memories and the often-fuzzy or even false details that accompany them.

Page 46: **Environmental factors can impinge upon our experience** See John K. Young, *Hunger, Thirst, Sex, and Sleep: How the Brain Controls Our Passions* (Lanham, MD: Rowman and Littlefield, 2012).

Page 47: **Those who were abused as children** See Douglas LaBier, "Why the Impact of Child Abuse Extends Well into Adulthood," *Psychology Today*, October 19, 2013, https://www.psychologytoday.com/blog/the-new-resilience/201310/ why-the-impact-child-abuse-extends-well-adulthood.

Page 47: **Human beings are liable to follow various forms of "herd mentality"** See the helpful summary of research by Stuart Jeffries, "Hands Up If You're an Individual," *The Guardian*, March 6, 2009, https://www.theguardian.com/lifeandstyle/2009/mar/07/ social-psychology-group-mentality.

Page 47: **I find the contemporary mindfulness movement** See the Greater Good Science Center's helpful overview, including a look at Jon Kabat-Zinn's Mindfulness-Based Stress Reduction (MBSR) program, which has helped many individuals in hospitals, schools, and prisons.

Page 47: **Mindfulness has become all the rage at companies in Silicon Valley** See Noah Shachtman, "In Silicon Valley, Mindfulness Is No Fad: It Could Make Your Career," *Wired*, June 18, 2013, http://www.wired.com/2013/06/ meditation-mindfulness-silicon-valley/.

Page 51: **Viktor Frankl counsels that in the face of darkness** Frankl expounds on this theory in "Logotherapy in a Nutshell," especially in the section "The Meaning of Suffering," in *Man's Search for Meaning*, 112ff.

Page 51: **A doctor who was experiencing severe depression** Recounted in *Man's Search for Meaning*, 113.

Page 55: ***New York Times* columnist David Brooks** *The Road to Character* (New York: Random House, 2014).

Page 56: **Only after a profound conversion did Saul** This section is influenced by Bernard Lonergan's discussion of the topic in *Method in Theology* (Toronto: University of Toronto Press, 1990), 105, 107.

Page 58: **"In a higher world it is otherwise, but here below"** From John Henry Newman, *An Essay on the Development of Christian Doctrine* (South Bend: Notre Dame Press, 1989), 1.7.

Page 58: **An authentic life . . . is open to the possibility of falling in love** From a talk given to religious women in 1981, "Rooted and Grounded in Love," quoted in Kevin Burke, SJ, "Love Will Decide Everything," *America*, November 12, 2007.

Page 58: **"As I opened the door which faced the city"** Arrupe's reflections originally appeared in *Recollections and Reflections of Pedro Arrupe, SJ* (Collegeville, MN: Michael Glazier, 1986) and are excerpted here from *Pedro Arrupe: Essential Writings*, selected and introduced by Kevin Burke, SJ (Maryknoll, NY: Orbis Books, 2004).

Page 59: **A young man who was later honored by the president of the United States** "Remarks of the President at 9/11 Museum Dedication," May 15, 2014, https://obamawhitehouse.archives.gov/the-press-office/2014/05/15/remarks-president-911-museum-dedication.

Page 59: **Welles Remy Crowther, the "man in a red bandanna"** Editorial Board, "The Man in a Red Bandanna," *New York Times*, May 15, 2014.

Page 60: **"Welles must have felt hugely fulfilled that day"** Quoted in Tim Heffernan, "That Masked Man," *Boston College Magazine*, Summer 2002. For more on Welles Crowther, see Tom Rinaldi, *The Red Bandana: A Life, a Choice, a Legacy* (New York: Penguin Press, 2016).

Page 61: **In Africa they say "a person becomes a person through other people"** Greg Boyle, *Tattoos on the Heart: The Power of Boundless Compassion* (New York: Free Press, 2010), preface.

Page 62: **Whom he describes as having a "privileged delivery system for giving me access to the gospel"** Ibid., 1.

Page 63: **"But, well . . . I don't eat"** Ibid., 149.

Page 64: **"So, son, tell me something,"** Ibid., 24.

Page 64: **"I was brought up and educated to give"** Ibid., 25.

Page 65: **Boyle tells the story of Carmen** Ibid., chap. 2.

Page 66: **"There is a longing in us all to be God-enthralled"** Ibid., 43, 44, 45.

Page 66: **One that Boyle remembers clearly is that of Ramiro** Ibid., 7.

Page 66: **"I am helpless to explain why anyone"** Ibid., 21.

Page 67: Such is the story of Katharine Drexel See the Vatican News Service biography used on the occasion of her canonization, available at www.vatican.va/news_services/liturgy/saints/ns_lit_doc_20001001_katharine-drexel_en.html.

Page 68: His response surprised her: "What about you? What are you going to do?" Pope Francis highlighted these questions of Pope Leo XIII's to Katharine Drexel in his homily at SS. Peter and Paul Basilica in Philadelphia, as reported in "Pope's Speech," (Philadelphia) *Morning Call*, September 26, 2015, www.mcall.com/news/local/mc-pope-basilica-speech-20150926-story.html.

Page 71: "The quality of mercy is not strained" *Merchant of Venice*, act 4, scene 1.

Page 72: "No one working with The Catholic Worker gets a salary" Dorothy Day, "Poverty and Precarity," in *By Little and by Little: The Selected Writings of Dorothy Day* (New York: Knopf, 2001), 107. Originally published in *The Catholic Worker*, May 1952.

Page 73: Luke, whom Paul describes as a physician Colossians 4:14.

Page 75: Like the person who sells all to buy a field in which there is a buried treasure Matthew 13:44.

Page 76: One of the traditional names for the devil is Lucifer The Latin comes from the Vulgate translation of the Bible by St. Jerome to render the Hebrew word *helel*, "shining one."

Page 77: We are asking the same question that St. Augustine asked *Confessions* 10.6. Augustine's question to God is, "When I love you, what do I love?" He points to what elicits desire for an object that transcends anything in the physical world.

Page 77: In his work Proslogion *Proslogion*, preface.

Page 77: In the words of the poet Rainer Maria Rilke, "the ever-greater One" Rainer Maria Rilke, "The Man Watching," trans. Edward Snow, in *The Book of Images* (New York: North Point Press, 1994), 211.

Page 78: God is, in the words of the theologian Michael Buckley Michael J. Buckley, *At the Origins of Modern Atheism* (New Haven, CT: Yale University Press, 1987), 360.

Page 78: Sin is a "failure to bother to love" James F. Keenan, SJ, *Moral Wisdom: Lessons and Texts from the Catholic Tradition* (Lanham, MD: Sheed and Ward, 2004), 55–63.

Page 78: **The theologians David Burrell and Stanley Hauerwas** David Burrell and Stanley Hauerwas, "Autobiography and Self-Deception," in *Truthfulness and Tragedy*, by Stanley Hauerwas, Richard Bona, and David B. Burrell (Notre Dame, IN: University of Notre Dame Press, 1977), 82–100.

Page 79: **The Jesuit priest Dean Brackley proposes an antidote** Dean Brackley, SJ: See an overview of his life and work at the Ignatian Spirituality website, at www.ignatianspirituality.com/ignatian-voices/ 21st-century-ignatian-voices/dean-brackley-sj.

Page 79: **He calls this antidote "downward mobility"** Dean Brackley, "Downward Mobility: Social Implications of St. Ignatius's Two Standards," *Studies in the Spirituality of Jesuits* 20, no. 1 (1988): 38. The editors point to Henri Nouwen's earlier use of the phrase "downward mobility" as the title of an article, presumably in his 1981 series in *Sojourners* magazine, now collected in the book *The Selfless Way of Christ: Downward Mobility and the Spiritual Life* (Maryknoll, NY: Orbis, 2011).

Page 81: **As we saw from Greg Boyle in chapter 4** *Tattoos on the Heart*, 1.

Page 83: **"What wrestles with us, how immense," writes Rilke** "The Man Watching."

Page 83: **"Ubuntu [is] the essence of being human"** http://www.tutufoundationuk.org/.

Page 83: **"We have become parts of people relating to parts of people"** *The Journey into Adulthood: Understanding Student Formation* (Boston: Division of University Mission and Ministry, Boston College, 2007), 7, http://www.bc.edu/ content/dam/files/offices/mission/pdf1/umm1.pdf.

Page 84: **Jean Vanier, the founder of L'Arche** See Jon Swinton's essay on Vanier's work, "An Embodied Theology," in which he quotes Vanier reflecting on his life's work, available at the website Jean Vanier: Transforming Hearts, www.jean-vanier.org/en/his_message/a_theology/a_embodied_theology.

Page 86: **What Nouwen discovered** See Arthur Boers's interview with him, "What Henri Nouwen Found at Daybreak," *Christianity Today*, October 3, 1994, http://www.christianitytoday.com/ct/1994/october3/4tb028.html, reflecting on Nouwen's book *The Road to Daybreak: A Spiritual Journey* (New York: Image Books, 1990).

Page 89: **"The real love of man must depend on practice"** From John Henry Newman, "Love of Relations and Friends," in *Parochial and Plain Sermons* (London: Longman, Green and Co., 1908), vol. 2, sermon 5.

Page 89: **According to the twelfth-century monk Aelred of Rievaulx** Aelred of Rievaulx, *Spiritual Friendship*, trans. Lawrence C. Braceland, ed. Marsha L. Dutton (Gethsemani, KY: Cistercian Publications, 2010).

Page 91: **Americans are obese at rates unheard of** On the obesity epidemic in the United States, driven by unhealthy fast food, sugary drinks, and other factors, see the report "Obesity" at PublicHealth.org: http://www.publichealth.org/public-awareness/obesity/.

Page 92: **The divorce rate remains at about half** "Marriage rates have declined steadily since the 1980s. Today they are lower than any other time since 1870, including during the Great Depression." Ana Swanson, "144 Years of Marriage and Divorce in the United States in One Chart," *Washington Post*, June 23, 2015, https://www.washingtonpost.com/news/wonk/wp/2015/06/23/144-years-of-marriage-and-divorce-in-the-united-states-in-one-chart/.

Page 92: **We are lonelier than ever** Jacqueline Olds and Richard S. Schwartz, *The Lonely American* (Boston: Beacon Press, 2010).

Page 93: **We had just read Aristotle's treatment of friendship** Books 8 and 9 of Aristotle's *Nicomachean Ethics* deal with friendship. See 1155a: "no one would choose to live without friends, despite having all the rest of the good things."

Page 96: **The ancient Greeks told a paradigmatic story of two friends, Damon and Pythias** The story is found in the writings of several classical authors: Aristoxenus (fourth century BC), Cicero and Diodorus Siculus (first century BC), and Valerius Maximus (AD first century), with some differences among the details. This version extrapolates from the little known about Pythagoras and speculates about his influence on the development of their friendship. It also speculates on the possible influence of Pythagoras on Plato's later understanding of tyranny.

Page 98: **The ancient Greek biographer Diogenes Laërtius** A third-century biographer of the ancient Greek philosophers attributes this saying to Aristotle (and it's usually attributed to Aristotle around the Internet), but the quote is not found in Aristotle's extended treatment of friendship in his *Nicomachean Ethics*. This idea sounds more like what Plato describes as Aristophanes's view of friendship in his *Symposium*, in which Aristophanes describes the myth of the *androgyne*, a creature cleaved in half such that one half of the creature constantly seeks out the other half.

Page 99: **"Tell me what company you keep," wrote Cervantes** Cervantes: *Don Quixote de la Mancha*, book 2, chap. 10: "Dime con quién andas, decirte he quién eres," says Sancho Panza, quoting a proverb and reflecting on what kind of person he must be to be following the crazy knight-wannabe Don Quixote around.

Page 101: **"Sometimes the frustrated will to meaning"** Frankl, *Man's Search for Meaning*, 107.

Page 103: **The writer Ronald Rolheiser calls "divine fire"** Ronald Rolheiser, *The Holy Longing: The Search for a Christian Spirituality* (New York: Image Books, 1999), 192ff.

Page 103: **Sexual passion, in some ancient mythologies** There are Greek stories such as that of Erebus sleeping with Night, giving rise to Ether (the heavenly light) and the earthly light; also Egyptian and Near Eastern myths. On sexual passion and jealousy, Homer's *Iliad* as well as the Dionysian rites of Rome.

Page 103: **One that had to be tamed by a disciplined will** Consider Plato's image of the charioteer with two horses, one of the will and one of the passions, in his *Phaedrus*.

Page 104: **Sales often correlated with sexualized advertising** See William M. O'Barr, "Sex in Advertising," *Advertising and Society Review 12*, no. 2 (2011), doi: 10.1353/asr.2011.0019.

Page 104: **Patterns of sexual desire related to the natural cycles of the seasons** Aristotle wrote a number of observations of the natural patterns of growth and of sexual congress, including observations that anticipate later, more scientific understanding of natural family planning, in his *History of Animals*, book 7.

Page 105: **More and more literature has underscored that observation, especially among young people** Laura Sessions-Stepp, *Unhooked: How Young Women Pursue Sex, Delay Love and Lose at Both* (New York: Riverhead Books, 2008); Michael Kimmel, *Guyland: The Perilous World Where Boys Become Men* (San Francisco: Harper Perennial, 2009); Joe S. McIlhaney Jr., Freda McKissic Bush, and Stan Guthrie, *Girls Uncovered: New Research on What America's Sexual Culture Does to Young Women* (Chicago: Northfield Publishing, 2012); Donna Freitas, *The End of Sex: How Hookup Culture Is Leaving a Generation Unhappy, Sexually Unfulfilled, and Confused about Intimacy* (New York: Basic Books, 2013).

Page 106: **That integration will involve periods of discerning relationships** See Jason King, *Faith with Benefits: Hookup Culture on Catholic Campuses* (New York: Oxford University Press, 2017).

Page 106: **The philosopher Blaise Pascal hints at in his comment** *Pensées* section 4, 277.

Page 108: **Queen Victoria . . . In an album that was a kind of writing therapy** See images of her album at the British Library website, at https://www.bl.uk/

collection-items/queen-victorias-album-consolativum-with-extracts-from-lord-alfred-tennysons-poem-in-memoriam-a-h-h.

Page 111: Be it a TV news network or a well-respected travel guide The Pew Research Center shows a rather dramatic decline in the way Americans access news: "The transformation of the nation's news landscape has already taken a heavy toll on print news sources, particularly print newspapers. But there are now signs that television news—which so far has held onto its audience through the rise of the internet—also is increasingly vulnerable, as it may be losing its hold on the next generation of news consumers." See "In Changing News Landscape, Even Television Is Vulnerable," September 27, 2012, http://www.people-press.org/2012/09/27/in-changing-news-landscape-even-television-is-vulnerable/.

Page 111: Such that our news feeds become exercises in confirmation bias See Tomas Chamorro-Premuzic's article "How the Web Distorts Reality and Impairs Our Judgement Skills," *The Guardian*, May 13, 2014, https://www.theguardian.com/media-network/media-network-blog/2014/may/13/internet-confirmation-bias. He writes that Paul Resnick and colleagues at the University of Michigan's School of Information recently noted that "collectively, these filters will isolate people in information bubbles only partly of their own choosing and the inaccurate beliefs they form as a result may be difficult to correct. Ironically, then, the proliferation of search engines, news aggregators and feed-ranking algorithms is more likely to perpetuate ignorance than knowledge."

Page 112: In a world that knows how to eradicate poverty I have in mind the UN Millennium Development goals (http://www.un.org/millenniumgoals/), the first of which is to eradicate poverty. Of that goal, the United Nations reports that the target of reducing extreme poverty rates by half was met five years ahead of the 2015 deadline, with one billion people lifted out of poverty since 1990. Still, there are some eight hundred million people still living in extreme poverty, and in the United States there are some forty-six million—enough to represent a population the size of Texas and New York combined.

Page 112: Economic forces consolidate wealth rather than expand its growth The top issue in the 2015 *Outlook on the Global Agenda* of the World Economic Forum is "deepening income inequality." Amina Mohammed writes, "In developed and developing countries alike, the poorest half of the population often controls less than 10% of its wealth. This is a universal challenge that the world must address. While it is true that around the world economic growth is picking up pace, deep challenges remain, including poverty, environmental degradation, persistent unemployment, political instability, violence and conflict. These problems, which are reflected in many parts of this report, are often closely related to inequality." Available at http://reports.weforum.org/ outlook-global-agenda-2015/wp-content/blogs.dir/59/mp/files/pages/files/ outlook-2015-a4-downloadable.pdf.

Page 112: **Either killed *in utero*** There are forty million to fifty million abortions per year globally, according to the World Health Organization. See Guttmacher Institute, "Facts on Induced Abortion Worldwide," http://www.who.int/reproductivehealth/publications/unsafe_abortion/ abortion_facts/en/.

Page 112: **Starved in infancy** According to the World Hunger Education Service, 3.1 million children die each year from hunger. See "World Child Hunger Facts," at www.worldhunger.org/world-child-hunger-facts/.

Page 112: **Why is there such prevalence of violence against women** The United Nations estimates that about one in three women worldwide experience some form of violence, usually by an intimate partner. See "Facts and Figures: Ending Violence Against Women," at http://www.unwomen.org/en/what-we-do/ ending-violence-against-women/facts-and-figures.

Page 112: **Why do so many people lack access to clean water or adequate sanitation** The United Nations estimated in 2013 that 783 million people worldwide did not have access to clean water and almost 2.5 billion did not have access to adequate sanitation. See the "World Water Day" website, at http://www.unwater.org/water-cooperation-2013/water-cooperation/ facts-and-figures/en/.

Page 114: **The Old Testament story of Abraham welcoming angels** Genesis 18:1–15. Compare the story of Lot and his wife in Genesis 19:2–3, as well as related stories in Judges 6:11–22 and Tobit 5:4.

Page 115: **Elsewhere, in the Torah, the command to** "When an alien [stranger] resides with you in your land, you shall not oppress the alien. The alien who resides with you shall be to you as the citizen among you; you shall love the alien as yourself, for you were aliens in the land of Egypt: I am the Lord your God." (Leviticus 19:33–34)

Page 115: **Similar stories pervade ancient literature** Ovid's story of Baucis and Philemon from *Metamorphoses* is about Zeus and Hermes coming to the earth as peasants and finding no one who will take them in but the aged couple. Like the widow of Zarephath, Baucis finds that her pitcher of wine does not run dry as she serves them. Because of their hospitality, they are allowed to escape to a mountain while Jupiter destroys the town with a flood. Similarly, Luke the Evangelist wrote the story of Paul and Barnabas arriving in Lystra and being received as gods, crying, "The gods have come down to us in human form!" (Acts 14:11) They called Barnabas and Paul "Zeus" and "Hermes," echoing Ovid's tale. And recalling Abraham's story of the three men, the author of the letter to the Hebrews wrote, "Do not neglect to show hospitality to strangers, for by doing that some have entertained angels without knowing it." (13:2)

Page 115: Reaching out to foreigners such as the Samaritan woman John 4:1–42. On the parable of the good Samaritan, see Luke 10:25–37. On the Roman centurion's servant, see Luke 7:1–10.

Page 115: Jesus called Paul to a *koinonia* The term is found in the New Testament seventeen times but none of them in the Gospels. The passages referred to are Acts 2:42, Romans 15:26, and 1 Corinthians 1:9 and 10:16.

Page 119: St. Ignatius offers an image of God "laboring" The image comes from the "Contemplation to Attain Love" in the Fourth Week of the Spiritual Exercises. Jesus' invitation to labor with him is from the "Call of Christ the King" from the Second Week.

Page 120: Walter Ong, a Jesuit priest and language scholar See his article "Yeast: A Parable for Catholic Higher Education," *America*, April 7, 1990.

Page 120: In his encyclical *Laudato Si'* Paragraph 66.

Page 121: For philosopher René Girard See his essay "Are the Gospels Mythical?" *First Things*, April 1, 1996, https://www.firstthings.com/article/1996/04/are-the-gospels-mythical.

Page 122: "God has created me to do Him some definite service" From Meditations on Christian Doctrine, March 7, 1848, found in *Meditations and Devotions of the Late Cardinal Newman* (New York: Longmans, Green, and Co., 1907), 299–302.

ABOUT THE AUTHOR

Tim Muldoon is the author of *The Ignatian Workout, Longing to Love, The Ignatian Workout for Lent*, and a number of other books. With his wife, Sue, he has cowritten three books about applying Ignatian spirituality to family life: *Six Sacred Rules for Families, The Discerning Parent*, and *Reclaiming Family Time*. A pastoral theologian, his research and teaching focus on the spirituality of the laity as well as marriage and family life. He has taught at Mount Aloysius College, Boston College, Washington Theological Union, and LaSalle University. He and Sue are the parents of three teenagers.

Ignatian Spirituality
www.ignatianspirituality.com

Visit us online to

- Join our E-Magis newsletter
- Pray the Daily Examen
- Make an online retreat with the *Ignatian Prayer Adventure*
- Participate in the conversation with the dotMagis blog and at **facebook.com/ignatianspirituality**